D1417889

Early Praise for *The Big Kid and Basketball ...*

I had to tell Tom that just getting through the first part
of the book without wanting to get it bound, drive to
the neighborhood where the bullying occurred, and
leaving a copy on every parent's doorstop was difficult.
This is a tremendous book about the effect of bullying
but it's also so much more. Tom takes you on this
journey where he looks at himself and how he tried,
and sometimes believed he failed, to coach young men
into believing in themselves. He explains how he led
teams to play from the heart for each other and how
that is the real measure of winning. It's Tom and his
family doing what they do best: live in gratitude and be
of service to yourself and others. That shines through
every page of this book. You'll be touched in ways I
won't ruin for you by spelling out. Read it and Enjoy.

Kristin Sunanta Walker
CEO, MHNR Network
Host, Mental Health News Radio

The big kid and basketball is a refreshing and honest memoir of a father's journey back to his own heart through coaching. This heartwarming story addresses parenthood, humility, faith, but most of all the power of vulnerability. Thomas Dahlborg presents a simple but beautiful story of how coaching his son's basketball team took him deeper into his own insecurities where he learned to face them head on. The purity of his words are truly encouraging and take the reader on a journey into his mind that reveals his truest love for his son. This book is about family, about altruism, and perseverance even when you think you aren't up for the task. The big kid and basketball is a story of hope and compassion for people of all abilities. We learn that when one focuses on their strengths instead of their weakness, entire new chapters can be written. This is a feel good read that every aspiring coach, teacher, or parent should be excited to pick up. If you are lucky enough to find your way to Thomas Dahlborg's heart which he so willingly reveals in his book, you will be touched by its sincerity.

Melanie Vann
Program and Advocacy Director
Mental Health News Radio

THE BIG KID ...

... and BASKETBALL

... and the lessons he taught his Father and Coach

Thomas H. Dahlborg, Sr.

The story of a child who overcame the impact of bullying through resilience, sports and love and how he taught his dad courage and determination.

Written by a healthcare leader, coach, husband and father.

Copyright © 2018 DHLG

Published by DHLG
Gorham, ME 04038
Phone: 207-747-9663
www.thebigkidandbasketball.wordpress.com
DahlborgHLG@gmail.com

ISBN-13: 978-1727019926
ISBN-10: 172701992X

The stories in this book are true. However, some names and identifying details have been changed to protect the privacy of all concerned.

Dedication

To my family. To my amazing bride who is the mother bear to us all, keeping us safe and helping us all to remain whole and healthy physically, mentally, emotionally and spiritually with the power of her fierce loving. To my daughters. Each beautiful inside and out. Each full of passion and drive. Each teaching, leading, serving, and loving others. To my son, the Big Kid, who leads with his heart – the Heart of the Lion. And to Gabriel, our papillon pup named for an angel, who loves us all unconditionally.

To all the coaches who are truly teaching, leading and most importantly caring for all those they are blessed to engage. Coaches like Kevin Doepp of Crack of the Bat, LLC, who understands that the skill of sport is important … and yet the skill of living life fully and in service to others is even more so.

To all those who have been bullied. You are not alone. We are here for you.

To all those who have bullied. We, too, are here for you.

And to the Ever-Living God, the Father – Son – Holy Spirit, for blessing us all with His majesty and ever-present love.

Table of Contents

Foreword

Life truly is incredible. All of us going through this journey … experience so much. We endure so much. Because of what we experience, we end up seeing the world in a certain way from our own perspective. I can look back and relive the memories that are in this book from my perspective, however the greatest part of this book is being able to view these memories through my dad's perspective.

Doing so brings tears to my eyes.

This book shows the heart of a dad who just wants "The Big Kid" to get a win. At times the "big kid" was me, at other times it was my sister, and at other times the "big kid" was a friend struggling with drugs or body image issues or the loss of a parent.

At one point or another, we have all been "The Big Kid."

What we go through as children often determines how we live and how we love when we are adults.

This book gives you a glimpse of what it truly means to be a coach and a parent, and how we need more adults like my dad. We need more people to give their hearts selflessly in the pursuit of helping all the "big kids" out there, so that they can grow up and love and help others.

We need to look at everyone in this world without pity, but rather with love. Everyone deserves a win. Let's all be the coach that helps them get it.

> Tommy Dahlborg
> The Big Kid

As a parent to the "Big Kid" you are forever trying to find the right words to somehow fix and undo the harm that bullies inflict on your child. This book shows the raw, first hand experiences that a coach (and father) and son (the Big Kid) share together and with others. A sometimes heartbreaking and emotional journey of trying to build up a child's character, self-esteem and self-worth in a world that is forever trying to tear them down. A book that reflects the lives of many battling "life" with losses: loss of loved ones, loss of friends and a loss of acceptance by others. An inspirational read that will have a positive impact on those who are struggling and help them re-establish a connection with the love of sport, love of community and love of one another.

Anything can be overcome with love.

> Darlene C. Dahlborg, RN
> Mother of the Big Kid

Chapter 1

The Beginning

"Mommy. Daddy. All the boys are next door. Can I go over and play too?"

My son Tommy (yes, a junior) was always a big kid. In fact, one of the reasons we had moved to the community of Gorham, Maine back in 2002 was because my son was … The Big Kid.

We had moved from Massachusetts to Maine in 1999, to a beautiful community on the coast, so that I could continue my career in healthcare at a local integrated delivery system.

Our home was beautiful, a builder's home, the neighborhood so quaint and the other homes so welcoming.

Oh, how looks can deceive.

Imagine the following happening to your child.

Tommy has several friends his age in the neighborhood.

Brendon, Tommy's best friend, lived next door.

"Of course, you can play next door, Tommy," we replied.

And as we kissed Tommy prior to his departure, we noticed his beautiful smile, the one deep dimple on the right side of his face, and his glistening blue eyes. Our boy. Our boy, who was born beautiful and with neurological challenges. Our boy, who each night we prayed would be okay, we prayed for strength, we prayed for guidance, and knew that no matter what we would give him the best life possible. Yes, our boy we were sending off to explore and to be with his friends.

"Have fun, T. Love you."

"Love you too, Dad."

Now, Tommy didn't just walk across our side yard and up to the door of our neighbor's home ... he skipped. He skipped with his slight leftward lean and awkward gate and yet he skipped with the glee of a young child about to be in community with those who know only love ... children. And at that, the unconditional love of friendship.

Three minutes later ...

"Mommy! Daddy! Why? Why can't I play with my friends? What did Brendon's mother mean? Please. Please. I want to play with my friends. Why?! What does she mean? Why can't I play?" Tommy cried.

"Tommy, what happened? What did Mrs. Williams say to you?"

"Brendon's mother, she said, she said, mom, dad, she said, 'Tommy, you are too big to come in and play. Go home!'"

And as we held Tommy, he held us, and our hearts broke.

Now imagine arriving at the bus stop in the morning to find that all the mothers, fathers and children are shunning you and your child because your child is "THE BIG KID".

Follow this up with a neighborhood block party where again you and your family are shunned because your child is "TOO BIG" to play with the other children his age.

As I said, beautiful homes and yet the people ....

"We are moving from here. We will no longer let these people hurt our Tommy!"

My bride (Doc) was right, as always. And we did, we moved. We moved to Gorham, to a smaller community, to a smaller house, away from the coast but also away from these people.

But why is this important to a basketball story?

Several years ago, my son wanted to play basketball. He was 8 years old at the time.

My heart sunk. Will he be accepted? Will he be mocked? Will he get hurt physically, mentally, emotionally?

We signed Tommy up for the Gorham Recreation League basketball program for eight-year olds. Little did we know what we were getting into.

Tommy was picked to play for a coach by the name of Jim Smith. Coach Smith.

Tommy had never played organized basketball, so all was new to him. And other than our oldest daughter Samantha playing soccer one season years ago in Taunton, Massachusetts and Tommy playing a little *organized* soccer (at the age when all 20 kids run to the ball regardless) and a bit of baseball, neither Doc nor I had much experience being parents of a child playing an organized sport.

We did remember Coach Smith from those soccer days as the coach with the great energy who would run and hop and jump and provide even more energy to children who probably did not need any more. He had a great way with children and was quite an athlete himself.

We would drop Tommy off at practice and on occasion watch the practice itself. But moreover, we would be at every game watching. Being the introvert, I was rather quiet. Being the extrovert, my bride was … well let's just say not so much.

Did I mention that my son was a big kid?

As I watched, I kept coming back to the fact that most of the boys were quicker, faster, and more agile than my son and my son was not necessarily having a great time out on the court.

And yet ...

And yet, God gave my son a gift.

My son was a big kid. And what can big kids excel at in basketball? That's right – rebounding. And to rebound really well one must learn to BOX OUT. Sexy? No. Grunt work? Perhaps. And yet, vital to a successful team at any level.

So, after viewing a few practices and a couple of games I realized that my son (the "big kid") could be positioned to be successful... by learning how to BOX OUT.

And why was this important?

Was it important that Tommy's team win the championship? I don't believe at that age they kept count of the score. (Although I am sure the boys themselves did.)

Was it important that I felt like a winner because my 8-year-old was a great ballplayer? I sure hope not.

The reason this was important was twofold: 1.) God gave Tommy a gift (a large frame), and 2.) Tommy deserved a win. With the bullying my son endured (that he endured with more maturity than most adults could or would have) he deserved a chance to feel good about himself and especially and specifically because he is the "big kid".

Did I mention my son's maturity?

Fast forward six years...

I just came from the home of Joanne Arnold, a professional trainer who has trained the likes of Ian Crocker, is a former Ms. Maine, Ms. Natural New England, and 2nd place finisher in the Ms. America bodybuilding contest, and is mentioned in John Douillard's book "Body, Mind and Sport". I had brought Tommy and Haylee (my youngest child) there to work on their core as they gear up for another season of activity. Joanne had met Tommy the day before and shared with me the following:

> *"Your son is amazing. To be a Freshman in High School and to lack any sense of machismo is astonishing. To care about doing things the right way rather than trying to simply 'dominate' is amazing. You should be very proud."*

And referencing back to those damaged people in that coastal community and their bullying of my son...

How often do you hear stories of bullies having been abused in the past?

Did my son become a bully? My gosh, my son is a hero. When his friend was being bullied on a school bus by two of the toughest children in the school my son stood up to each until they each backed down and then above that, the next day he reconnected with the two children who were bullying and made sure they were okay too.

When his sisters are hurting, or our puppy is sick, or Doc or I are upset or arguing (yes, on occasion we argue) who is the first to show how much he cares? You get one guess.

When I am heading off to work or to the gym or to the store, no matter what he is doing who will jump up and run over and give me a big hug? When it is bed time or when he wakes up in the morning who always comes over for a kiss on the cheek and/or a hug? Yes, the "big kid" … my son Tommy.

Tommy has become the definition of empathic. Perhaps he should become a doctor and lead the charge to bring empathy back into healing? (But that is another story for another day.)

So back to eight-year-olds playing basketball and boxing out.

As I said, it was now time for Tommy to get a win. It was time to put to good use God's gift to Tommy (his body).

One day after school and shortly after the start of the basketball season Tommy and I went outside to the street where we have our own basketball hoop. We passed, we dribbled, we shot and while we did so I described Larry Bird. I talked about Larry, who was one of my favorite Boston Celtic players, but not as good as Tommy Heinsohn of course. (I was named after Tommy Heinsohn so admittedly I am a bit biased). I shared how Larry would go home to French Lick, Indiana during the off season each year and learn another skill to add to his repertoire. (I don't believe I used the term repertoire at that time though with my 8-year-old son.) I shared how Larry Bird was not blessed with great speed, vertical leaping ability, or quickness, and yet he is considered one of the best to ever play the game because he got the most out of the gifts God had provided to him. I mentioned how Larry would learn and do whatever he needed to in an effort to position his team to win.

We then talked about Charles Barkley. I shared that God had blessed Charles with a large frame. I then described how Charles Barkley played. How he was nicknamed the "bread truck" and how he used his body to "box out" and get rebounds and help his team win.

I then showed Tommy how to get in position to box out, how he "owned" the semi-circle of space between him and the hoop, and the basic mechanics of boxing out. Together we saw how much easier it was to get the ball after a missed shot when we boxed out the correct way, with right action, and I showed Tommy how his gift from God, his body, was so incredibly perfect for this important aspect of the game of basketball.

We did this for an hour or so and then did it again a couple of afternoons later. Each time with me reminding Tommy that God gave him a gift and all we were doing was using God's gift to him to honor God, achieve a goal, and have some fun.

The Friday evening before Tommy's next game (which happened to be at 8am on Saturday morning) I could barely sleep. (Tommy slept soundly). I was so anxious. Was I doing the right thing? Did I put too much pressure on my son? Did I teach the box out correctly? Will Coach Smith be upset that I taught Tommy this move? Most importantly, am I doing the right thing for the right reason – again, right action - and will Tommy be happy?

It is now shortly after 8am Saturday morning and Tommy takes his turn on the court. The quicker boys are flying up and down the court. They are laughing and joking and throwing up shot after shot and Tommy is struggling to keep up. Doc is cheering him on and I am biting my tongue trying to keep quiet so that I do not impede what Coach Smith is doing.

Soon Tommy is running near the sidelines and just loud enough so that only he can hear I say, "Tommy, remember your special gift from God, box out."

Tommy looked up at me and I saw a very small but noticeable twinkle in his eye and that wonderful dimple that only appears when he smiles. "Box out," I whispered again.

Tommy's team is on offense. Tommy positions himself in the paint and I see him get in box out position. (Sure, glad at this age they do not call "3-seconds"!) He backs himself into one of the quicker and more aggressive boys on the other team and makes contact. He then remains attached to this boy like glue. Not necessarily a natural thing to do for a shy 8-year-old boy. Tommy's teammates dribble left. They dribble right. They dribble to the baseline and then back out to half court. (Ever notice how much dribbling takes place in 8-year-old boys' basketball?) And then a boy finally takes a shot.

Tommy is in good box out position. The quick aggressive boy cannot get around him. The ball hits the rim, and then the backboard. And then…you guessed it…Tommy has boxed out well and gets the rebound. Now of course being a 39-year-old man at the time I respond with stoic resolve. Well, actually tears begin to flow freely down my cheeks as my boy, the "big kid", grabs his first rebound, pivots, and passes the ball to a teammate.

Okay, beginners' luck, right?

Now down the defensive end. Tommy gets in the paint again. He finds an offensive player (again with more quickness and agility and this time more height too). Tommy proceeds to get between this boy and the basket, he bends his knees, and he backs into this boy and starts to move this boy backwards. Tommy creates a 4-foot half arc of space between himself and the hoop. A shot from the other team. A miss. Tommy grabs the rebound. Pivots hard. Makes an outlet pass to a teammate and they are off. So, of course again I am calmly watching this happen. (Actually no, I am weeping again. Men weep at basketball games, don't they?)

Tommy ends up with 8 rebounds for the game. Yes, I counted. And better yet, his dimple reappears as he shares with Doc and I how he boxed out and got rebounds and helped his team win.

His team win? I don't know. Again, I cannot even recall if the score was kept for the game. But there definitely was a win this day. My son got his win. My son the "big kid" got his win.

The ride home we talked about how he boxed out and got rebounds. Walking into the house we talked about the number of rebounds. At lunch we relived the first rebound. The second rebound. The third rebound. We told Tommy how very proud of him we are. Not for the rebounds but for helping his team do well. And throughout these conversations I kept saying to God ... "thank YOU".

That afternoon Tommy asked me to play basketball with him again. We went outside, and we did not discuss boxing out. Mostly we simply and quietly passed the ball to one another and took turns shooting.

Does life get any better?

Box out, rip it, clear out

A few days later we went back outside to play again, and I shared with Tommy my father's old saying: "box out, rip it, clear out". My father to this day remains a great basketball player. Me on the other hand, I was perfect for teaching boxing out and rebounding. No one misses shots more often than I do so there are plenty of rebounding opportunities for my son.

So back to "box out, rip it, clear out".

What does it mean? Essentially it serves as a reminder. Everyone on the court wants the ball. Everyone. To achieve the goal of getting the ball one must be in good position – box out. Then one must be prepared to grab the ball and rip it away from others who also want that ball – rip it. And then one must ensure that no one can grab that ball away from you once you have it in hand – clear out. Watch old films of Dave Cowens from the Boston Celtics. No one did it better. (Don't tell Tommy Heinsohn I said that.)

So, I would shoot the ball, I would yell "box out, rip it, clear out", I would miss, and Tommy would box out, rip it and clear out. Over and over we did this. And we laughed. We laughed at how poor a shooter I am. We laughed at the silliness of me repeating over and over "box out, rip it, clear out", and we laughed because we were father and son just playing and having fun together outside in the sun. To answer my own question: yes, life can't get any better.

The next Saturday morning Tommy has another game. The stands are packed. Yes, for 8-year-old Saturday morning recreational basketball. Not being comfortable in crowds I spot a folding chair on the sidelines and leave Doc and my two daughters to take the seat all by myself.

The game begins, and Tommy is starting. He is running and smiling as he charges down the court behind the other nine players to get on defense. But with all of the dribbling he has plenty of time to get in his favorite box out position. Shot goes up and misses. Tommy boxes out another boy, rips the rebound down, clears out so no one can take it away and passes to his speedy teammate. All the while I am repeating to myself (hopefully so no one else could hear) "box out, rip it, clear out, box out, rip it, clear out, box out, rip it, clear out". This goes on for the remainder of the game and Tommy walks away with 13 rebounds and even better…walks over to me on the sideline with a smile from ear to ear. "I did it dad! I boxed out, I ripped it and I cleared out! I did it! Are you proud of me?"

Am I proud of him? My god. Am I proud of my son for boxing out? Am I proud of my son for ripping the ball? Am I proud of my son for clearing out? What is the right answer to share with an 8-year-old? What is the right answer to share with myself?

I want to say: "Tommy I am so proud of you for the person you are. I am so proud of how you have shown a maturity and heart in your very young life that many adults could never understand. I want to hold my boy and let him know that I am so proud of him and it has nothing to do with basketball. I want him to know that me being proud of him is so very minor. Him loving himself and knowing he is blessed and loved by God that is far more important. I am so proud of my boy. My boy the lion. And it has nothing to do with basketball."

Chapter 2

A Reputation

Do I say all of this? No. Do I say any of this? No. I wish I did, but no. Rather I look at my boy, the boy with the huge heart, the lion, and simply smile and say, "Yes, Tommy. I am so proud of you. You worked hard. You helped your team. You did great. I am so very proud of you. I love you."

Eight-year-old boys Saturday morning Gorham recreational basketball has approximately ten games in each season. And for the last five games of Tommy's first season he excelled.

For these last five games Tommy dominated as he continued to learn and grow. His technique, footwork and most of all … desire … desire to rebound and help his team continued to grow and improve. Tommy's desire to box out, rip it, clear out and distribute the ball to his teammates grew with each practice, with each game.

Tommy continued to combine the gifts he received from God, with his knowledge of the game, and this powerful desire to be of service to his team. Each game his ability to anticipate when a shot would go up, where a rebound would come off the rim, and the direction an opposing player is likely to move to get the rebound improved to the point where he was being compared by coaches and parents alike to a young Dave Cowens by year end.

And best of all, he smiled, and he laughed. For the first time in his life Tommy truly felt part of a team, of a community. And he had fun and he had his win. The boy "too big to play with the other kids" had his win.

A Reputation

Tommy also developed a reputation, and no not a reputation due to the adverse impacts of being bullied (by adults in Tommy's case), but another type of reputation.

Slowly at first, like the first ripple of a pebble penetrating a pristine crystal lake, and then greater and greater as the ripples became waves, we began to hear coaches (coaches of other teams) call out to their own players ...

> *"Boys! Rebound like number 15!"* or comment to those nearby *"Boxing out at 8 years old?"* or huffing *"How many rebounds does that kid have?"* or (my personal favorite) *"I can't even get my High School basketball team to box out!"*

Yes, rebounds and boxing out. Coaches of competing teams, coaches of older teams, and of course Tommy's own coach all began to know Tommy as the eight-year-old boy who could AND would box out and rebound. The kid who did the important things to help his team.

Tommy Dahlborg, the kid who would rebound.

Riding home after Tommy's last game of the season the latest volley of feedback from coaches still rang in our ears:

> *"Wow ... I wish you played for me!", "I have never seen anyone attack the boards like you!"* and *"You are quite a ball player, I will be keeping an eye out for you."*

Quite the juxtaposition from "you are too big to play with other kids".

And as I looked in the rear-view mirror, I could see Tommy smiling again from ear to ear as he relived his latest game, his past season, his win.

And yes, I make like Dick Vermeil and cry and cry and cry.

Chapter 3

The Coach

After the last game of the season, Coach Smith approached me on the sidelines. He shared similar feedback about Tommy with Doc and I and then he really surprised me when he asked, "Will you coach with me next year?"

Never short on words I responded very eloquently with … "Huh?"

Coach? Me? I am an extreme introvert. I have played team sports (close to twenty years ago) but never coached. I know very little of the intricacies of coaching. I know very little of coaching theory. I know very little of basketball rules and regulations, X's and O's, proper positioning and so forth. I simply love my son and wanted him to get a "win".

So, considering all I don't know and realizing that the next season doesn't start for another 10 months (enough time for us all to have forgotten about this conversation) I respond …

"I will definitely consider coaching with you Jim. It could be a lot of fun."

Needless to say, I did not sleep that night. All I thought about was the sheer terror of me stepping outside my comfort zone to coach.

And that was my introduction to coaching. This is how IT all started. Teaching my son to box out led me down the pathway to coaching. The way I see it, my son got me a job, a job that does not pay a nickel, but a job nonetheless … one of the most important jobs there is. One I am most proud of. One in which my son teaches me more than he will ever realize.

Pathway to coaching

Fast forward 9 months…Tommy brings home a Gorham recreation form which shows that it is once again time to sign up for boys' recreational basketball. And guess what? Tommy had such a fun season last year he wants to play again. Yes! Absolutely wonderful. He has continued to practice. To learn the game. To grow. And to love the sport.

And who could remember a 2-minute conversation 9 months ago about coaching? No worries. Let's sign the paperwork, send it in to the Gorham Rec Department and look forward to another fun season of watching Tommy do something he very much enjoys and does so very well.

George Orwell was right

Now how did he find me? How did Coach Smith get my E-mail address? George Orwell, how did you know?

Shortly after Tommy submitted his form to play basketball again I received an E-mail from Coach Smith. He reiterated his request that I help him coach the boys' basketball team this year.

What is he an elephant? (Elephants never forget, right?)

Reading the E-mail, I felt the same panic I had felt 9+ months prior. No way! I cannot coach! I don't want to coach! I have never coached. And parents? What about those stories I read about parents? I don't want to have to deal with that! I don't know how to deal with that! No way! There has got to be a good excuse for why I cannot, why I should not, and why I would not coach.

Looking in the mirror I had to admit to myself. I was scared. Scared of failing; scared of looking foolish; scared of being humiliated; scared of not being able to help these boys; scared of losing and being blamed; scared of dealing with parents; scared of embarrassing my son; scared of embarrassing my family; and unfortunately, most importantly to me at that time, scared of embarrassing myself. I simply love my son and wanted him to get a "win". Why do I have to grow and mature and work through my own issues and growing edges? And why do I have to do so in public?

What did I do to deserve this?

So of course, I replied to Jim's E-mail with a resounding … "Yes, I am happy to help coach."

I must be an idiot. I cannot do this! Someone please help me. God help me.

Chapter 4

The E-mail

Fast forward a few years ...

> *"You are the worst coach ever! I have never seen such a sloppy practice. And the game? Pathetic! Unprepared. No direction! Why do you waste my son's time?!"*

Have you ever read an E-mail that made you gasp?

A few days prior to receiving the message above, I had asked the seemingly innocuous question of Brian Boxswain, a parent of one of my players, "How did the boys do at the last game?"

I had asked the question because I had been out of town on business and could not be there.

As a reminder ...

This is not a D-1 college basketball program where we are seeking millions in revenue and fighting tooth and nail to make the Sweet Sixteen or better in the NCAA Tourney commonly known as March Madness.

This is not high school basketball where winning the championship can save your job and builds your reputation for further coaching pursuits and young men strive to gain the attention of college scouts.

This is not middle school basketball where parents are pushing for their kids to get playing time and exposure, so they are well positioned for high school ball.

This is 8th grade recreation basketball where during the winter months children can get some exercise, learn basketball fundamentals, learn how to play as a team, learn some life lessons for off the court, and play a game they enjoy.

Am I a basketball expert? No. I am a parent who loves his son and at least initially simply wanted him "the big kid" to get a win. And now a parent who simply wants to help.

Did I play basketball in college? No. I was a football player (until achieving what is known as the unhappy triad (and then some) by tearing three ligaments and both the lateral and medial meniscus (cartilage) in my right knee while on the gridiron).

Did I play high school basketball? No.

Did I play in a recreation basketball league like these boys? Yes.

Back in my day in my hometown of Brockton, Massachusetts those of us not playing high school basketball for any reason (my reason was I was not good enough) but still enjoyed the game and belonged to a church parish or temple played what was known as "Church Ball".

Am I named after the greatest player in basketball history? Yes – Tommy Heinsohn. (Remember what I said about bias).

Am I now officially the worst coach ever? Could this person who I respect greatly be right?

Chapter 5

The First Practice

Back to coaching for the first time

I said "yes" to coaching with Jim? What was I thinking?

Over the next few weeks I tried to get every penny out of Google I could. I searched and read everything I could on coaching basketball. "Tips for basketball coaches"; "Designing basketball plays"; "Coaching young men"; "Basic defenses"; "Basic offenses"; "Basic full court presses"; "Basic press breaks"; "Basic drills"; and so much more. By the way the "basic" aspect was more for me than for the boys.

Sleep did not come easily for me over those few weeks as the date of the first practice came nearer and nearer.

By the time the first practice arrived the bags under my eyes were larger than those mega golf bags you see Phil Mickelson use to carry his 8 wedges and 14 drivers ... and the dark circles under my eyes were darker than the Cave of the Winds in Colorado Springs after you turn your flashlight off. And my gut? I looked 8 months pregnant due to the stress induced bloating.

No doubt Mike Krzyzewski looks and feels like this prior to Duke's first practice each year. Right?

Okay, it is the evening of the first practice. Monday night, 7:00pm, at the Village School gym, an old, small gymnasium, with dirty slippery floors, and lots of bright fluorescent lights.

I wonder if the fluorescent lights will show off my bags, dark circles and pasty skin.

I can feel my nerves. The pit of my stomach is both hollow and enlarged at the same time and grumbling nonstop. My hands are literally shaking and of course clammy. Tommy on the other hand is pumped and ready to go.

"Come on dad…we are going to be late."

It is 6:30pm.

"Let's go dad!"

It takes less than 5 minutes to get there.

"Dad, where are you? Come on…I don't want to be late! Come on!"

Okay, we are finally in the car and on our way to our first practice with me as an Assistant Coach. Tommy is pumped for the season. I am dreading it.

We arrive at the Village School and immediately I need to find the bathroom. I had heard the great Bill Russell used to vomit before every game. Do you think he did so before every practice?

I walk out of the bathroom and into the brightly lit (remember fluorescent bulbs) hallway and make my way to the gym.

Lots of kids and parents are in the hallway. I must not make eye contact, or I might have to speak or worse they will see my pale skin, bloated belly, dark circles, and hand tremor. (Didn't you know that closing your eyes (or in this case not making eye contact) made you invisible?)

Phew, I made it to the door. It worked. I was stealth. Who needs Harry Potter's invisibility cloak?

Hmmm…I see a window in the door. Let's take a look. Lots of boys running and jumping and laughing and shooting and missing. Missing? I can do this. Can't I?

Tommy had just changed into his basketball sneakers and was now joining the boys with a big smile on his face. The Big Kid is ready to play. Why was I ever concerned about my boy? Tommy is courageous. I must be too.

I take a deep breath, open the door and step into a percussion of dribbling, laughing, screaming, and more laughing.

Looking to the left I see Coach Smith as enthusiastic and energetic as ever. He is running, jumping, dribbling, screaming, laughing and playing.

I slowly, reluctantly, make my way over to him.

"Hey Tom, great to see you!" And then he is off. Chasing the boys. Back to running, jumping, dribbling, screaming, laughing and playing.

I see to my right a couple of more adults. Other Assistant Coaches perhaps? Oh great…more people to embarrass myself in front of. Ugh!

I know I should have been thinking, "Oh great…more help…less pressure on me." But nope, clearly, I am not wired that way.

I make note that one of these adults is Bill Wright. Bill is an excellent baseball coach with that quiet confidence, smooth voice, and great command over kids that makes you say, "He was born to coach". He also knows his baseball X's and O's and has a son who is also quite talented at baseball, basketball and golf.

Bill looks at me and then quickly goes back to his conversation. He must have seen my pale face, bloated belly, dark circles and hand tremor.

God, why am I here?

Coach Smith finally blows his whistle (I need a whistle) and calls all the kids and the three assistant coaches into the middle of the basketball court. Yes, three assistant coaches. Bill Wright, a fellow with an easy smile named Pete Sampras, (no not that Pete Sampras), and me. Coach Smith introduces himself and begins to talk about ... well, I'll be honest ... I have no idea what he said as all I could focus on was "How do I introduce myself? What do I say? How will I gain the respect of these boys? How will I gain the respect of the other coaches? I want to go home!"

Eventually Jim (Coach Smith) turns to me clearly wanting me to introduce myself. At this point I am in a shear state of panic.

I know. Pathetic.

So, I muster up all my courage and say with a weak and timid voice, "Ah, hi, I am Coach T-T-Tom".

You may wonder why I opted to say Coach Tom instead of Coach Dahlborg. Well, I know that when I am nervous (and even sometimes when I am not) I have trouble saying my last name "Dahlborg". (The Boston accent doesn't help). And when that happens I am usually asked to repeat it and it simply gets worse. So being the brilliant thinker that I am I avoided my last name and said Coach T-T-Tom instead. Yes, brilliant!

Well, Coach Smith looked at me like I had fifteen heads. (Yes, heads with pale skin and dark circles under the eyes but 15 none-the-less.) He shakes his head and moves on to Coaches Wright and Sampras.

By the way, they had no problem saying their LAST names and a few words of wisdom.

Ugh! I want to go home now.

I cannot remember much more from that first practice. Yes, I remember flubbing my name and making a fool of myself. I remember Coach Wright ignoring me. I remember Coach Smith shaking his head and thinking that he should not have asked me to assist him. (Didn't I tell you I could read minds?)

And I remember Coach Sampras … Coach Sampras smiling at me and simply talking calmly to me. A calming influence from God? Perhaps.

So, of course on the way home being the great father that I am I focused 100% on my son. I asked him about his experience at practice. I responded with great words of wisdom. Some might say John Wooden-esque words. We laughed. We went for ice cream. One of those father-son nights they make Hallmark cards and movies about that neither of us will ever forget.

Well, actually none of that happened. I wish it did. I really wish I was a better father…a better man. But no…I was not.

I may have asked Tommy about his experience at practice, but I have no idea what he replied. All I could think about that ride home, that night, all night, the next day, and for days after was how much I humiliated myself. My worst nightmares about coaching that I dreamt for 9+ months came true (and were even worse than I had feared).

"God, why can't I be like Coaches Smith, Wright and Sampras?" I don't belong coaching. I just want to be alone. Alone on the sideline watching my son get his "wins".

Chapter 6

The Second Practice

It is the following Wednesday and we have another practice. For the past 7 days I have thought non-stop about my humiliation. At work. In the car. At home. I have thought about how I screwed up. How I embarrassed my son.

So of course, my face is paler (is that possible?), my belly is more bloated (perhaps 9 months pregnant?), the circles under my eyes are darker (you know that sexy black color you see on certain Harleys? Well, the black under my eyes was nothing like that).

So, here we go again…

"Come on dad…we are going to be late."

It is 6:30pm.

"Let's go dad!"

It takes 5 minutes to get there.

"Dad, where are you?"

"Come on…I don't want to be late!"

"Come on!"

One guess where I am … (Don't tell Bill Russell that I didn't even make it to the gym).

Eventually I make it to the car. My sweatpants are so tight that I feel like I am about to explode. Picture a man 5' 11 ½" (nope…never made it to 6 feet), weighing 230 lbs., with a belly protruding way past his chest with not a six pack but rather a keg above his waist line feeling like the weight of the world is on his shoulders as he seeks to emulate the courage his son has shown since day one.

As we drive to the practice Tommy is talking about his jump shot, working on his dribble, how he wants to use my moves (my moves?), and how he can't wait to get there.

I am thinking about…yup…my gut, twisting, turning, aching, and swelling.

We arrive at practice and I remember to take a big breath and walk into the gym.

Again, it is loud and bright, and I see Coach Smith, Coach Wright, and Coach Sampras. I am here because? (Well, I am here for my son). But I mean really, how many coaches do you need for 12 boys playing recreation basketball?

Coach Smith blows his whistle, instructs the boys to each grab a basketball and then to form two lines, each at half court, one line facing one basketball hoop and the other facing the other basketball hoop. Ah, layup drill! I know this one. I can do this. But wait, I am not to get in a line. I am a coach, yes, one of four, but still a coach, right? What do I do?

Quietly I step off to the side and watch the boys, each one at a time, dribble to one hoop and take a layup and then grab their own rebound (ah yes, rebounding), get in the next line, and dribble to the other end and take another layup. Coach Smith is yelling words of encouragement. So is Coach Wright. Coach Sampras is quieter but definitely engaged. And here am I … watching.

Oh wait, Tommy's turn. Now this is why I am really here, right? To watch and support my son. He dribbles with his right hand to the first hoop. He throws it up. Off the backboard and … misses. He runs, he grabs his own rebound and he heads to the next line. Some of the boys are snickering at his miss. But most are too busy dribbling and getting ready for their next turn. Tommy is unfazed. My son is … smiling. He had a "fail" (as the kids would say) … and he is unfazed.

I have so much to learn from my son.

Tommy's next turn. He dribbles with his right hand, drives to the hoop, throws the ball up and IT'S GOOD! Yeah!! (I am jumping on the inside and smiling on the outside.) Tommy grabs the ball after it passes through the netting and heads to the next line. The boys who made fun of him for missing the first time don't appear to have noticed that he got it in this time. BUT I NOTICED. "Great shot, Tommy!"

This goes on for another 5 – 10 – 15 hours … um … I mean minutes.

Coach Smith eventually brings the boys to half court and discusses … actually, I have no idea what he discusses. Where is the bathroom?

Okay I am back.

Coach Smith has the boys lined up working on chest passes and bounce passes. Easy right? Not so much. Coach Smith is great at focusing on the basics. The boys (like most young boys) want to run and dribble and shoot. But God bless them, they stick with it and over time the majority develop a nice chest pass and an adequate bounce pass. My role? I am watching.

Coach Wright (who clearly knows his stuff) then teaches the boys another intricacy of the game: "How to set a screen." And the boys run that drill over and over. And then it is scrimmage time.

"Scrimmage! Who wants to SCRIMMAGE?!" Coach Smith shouts. Wow…have you ever seen stampeding bison in old cowboy movies? That is what these boys looked like heading to center court all ready to "run and gun" (as my father would say). The energy and enthusiasm…just wonderful!

20 minutes of boys running, sweating, dribbling, shooting (and occasionally passing) later and practice is over and we (I) survived.

Humiliated? No...at least I don't think so.

Non-existent? Pretty much.

Embarrassed? Definitely...but at least not humiliated this time.

On the other hand...

Have you seen old films of Red Auerbach? Red was the greatest professional basketball coach ever and happens to have been the commencement speaker at my graduation from Stonehill College back in 1988.

Red was a heavy-set balding man who commanded respect from some of the greatest basketball players ever: Bill Russell (greatest center), Bob Cousy (greatest point guard), Tommy Heinsohn (well...you know what I think of Heinsohn), Sharman, Jones, Jones, etc.

As a coach it is critical to be respected.

Did these boys respect me? Absolutely not. I was the fat guy who couldn't say my own name.

Do these boys listen to me? No. I was the pale guy who was so unsure of himself.

Did these boys take seriously any improvement opportunity I shared with them? No way. Coaches Smith and Wright are the experts.

I was the just the fourth coach … the one standing on the sideline.

And I was embarrassing my son.

Chapter 7

The Snake

Looking back, I recall my son looking at me during this time period (a time when I felt so small) like I still knew it all.

"Tommy don't you see your father embarrassing himself on the court?"

My son (the boy who was not allowed to play with the other kids because he was too big) giving me a hug and kiss at bedtime after each practice and thanking me for being HIS coach.

My son (the "big kid") asking me for advice or for my thoughts on basketball.

My son. I am so blessed.

Funny how God works…at your low points by His Grace He brings to you His paraclete in the form of a boy (a Son).

Thank you, God.

Thank you, Tommy.

I wish I had been able to recognize this back then. I wish I was able to let Tommy's love for me wash over me and cleanse me of all my demons. Ah, the wisdom of hindsight and age...

"I'VE LEARNED THAT PEOPLE WILL FORGET WHAT YOU SAID, PEOPLE WILL FORGET WHAT YOU DID, BUT PEOPLE WILL NEVER FORGET HOW YOU MADE THEM FEEL." – Maya Angelou

But back at that time I did not allow the love in. I was still in fight or flight (actually, just flight) mode ... "countdown" mode: Okay...two practices down. How many more to go? When is the first game? The last game? Can't end soon enough.

One Small Win for Dad

The league we were playing in has specific rules. Each player must play an even number of minutes and those boys who played on "travel" teams cannot play back to back periods (1/2 quarters) unless that is your only option (meaning everyone else has played).

Easier said than done.

If you want to watch WWE in live action without having to purchase a ticket, watch coaches contest one another's substitutions during a 9 & 10-year-old Saturday morning boys' basketball league. This can get very competitive and quite ornery.

After a few games of Coach Smith putting his lineup together, for some reason he asked me to make out the next one.   Why me?

Well … I am a self-taught Microsoft Excel Geek. So, the first thing I do (after reading the substitution rules again) is open an Excel workbook and go to work.

Hmmm … each player must play an even number of minutes and boys who play on "travel" teams cannot play back to back periods unless that is your only option. Hmmm … How can we leverage the rules and our team make-up in a way that best positions the boys and the team for success while honoring these rules?

After many hours of "playing" with Excel I develop a lineup that I believe will meet all the requirements of the league, ensure equal playing time, and best position our team to win. And in the process, I come up with a tool in which each week I can plug in the roster and arrive at an optimal lineup regardless of who we are playing and which of our players show up. Yes!

I decide to call it … the "snake".

Not Kenny Stabler snake-worthy but for an Excel geek pretty cool none-the-less.

What the snake does within Excel is it automatically populates each periods lineup evenly and by moving for example the 2nd best player to the 5thposition (so still in the starting lineup) it allows for our best players to play both side by side with our other best players at the beginning and end of games (through the snake movement of the lineup) while also giving everyone equal playing time.

Brilliant ... right?

Actually, quite simple once the rule was simplified in my mind and the model was built.

Now time for the first test.

I send Coach Smith my suggested lineup for the next game and he responds with a resounding:

"Thanks." (Did I mention that I am a Myers-Briggs 'F'?)

Okay ... could be worse right?

Game Time

During games Coach Smith is up, walking the sidelines, yelling instructions and encouraging the kids and the team. Coach Wright is at the scorer's table, "keeping the book" (game stats), while also sharing instructions with the kids on the bench. Coach Sampras is typically sitting on the bench (actually, on a folding chair during home games) and I am always down at the far end of the bench taking notes.

But this time I have a job. I am now responsible for ensuring that the lineup is adhered to. So, I have my copy of the lineup I had suggested to Coach Smith and I am watching the clock and telling the boys when it is their time to go into the game (according to the rules and the "snake").

Hmmm ... rules ... snake? What could go wrong?

Just what my gut needed, more pressure.

We are playing against a team whose coach (Stan Bellows) I remember well from Tommy's Cal Ripken baseball (similar to Little League) experiences. He is a short fellow with a big smile that is seen far too rarely. He is fiery and when he doesn't like a call in a Cal Ripken baseball game is quick to yell, scream, accuse, and truly go "off the deep end". (I wonder where that phrase came from?)

The basketball game is very close, and we are now moving into the final period. The snake is working well. The kids all have equal playing time. Tommy is playing as much as everyone else. He is rebounding and making solid passes and appears to be enjoying himself. Our best players are now in a position to go back in to finish the game. And then it happens...

Coach Bellows starts yelling: "What is going on here?!?!? These boys cannot go back in!!!! This is against the rules!!! This is bull$@^!!!!!"

And of course, I immediately go to the place of:

"Did I screw this up? Is the snake methodology wrong? Did I make a mistake?"

While these things are going through my mind Coach Wright calmly walks over to me and requests the lineup I developed. He looks at it and steadily walks over to Stan and says:

"This is the lineup. It is within the rules. All the boys have had equal playing time. Take a look."

"I don't give a $@^! about a piece of paper. This is bull$@^!!! Just play the f@$%in' game and then I am going to the league!"

(I told you this was WWE-lite).

We play the rest of the game and with our two best players back in and Tommy rebounding we win the game handily. Our boys are excited. Everybody lines up for handshakes…except for Coach Bellows who is still steaming. I am sure glad he doesn't know that I made out the lineup.

After the game Coach Smith and Coach Wright talk to the team, share their thoughts on what worked well and what we can improve on and then dismisses the team.

And that is it … or so I thought.

A few days later the league commissioner sends an E-mail to Coach Smith who forwards it along to me.

Subject line: "From league office".

Ugh....

"The League has found the lineup used by this team to be in accordance with the rules and recommends that **all** teams utilize this type of line up to ensure equal and fair playing time."

Phew … but too bad … now every team has my strategy.

Darn it.

Perhaps I should have trademarked the "snake"?

Back to the proverbial drawing board aka Excel.

Chapter 8

Am I Coaching?

I have a number of pet-peeves with one in particular having to do with basketball is what is called "giving up baseline". It drives me crazy when watching a game at any level to see a player beat the defender on the baseline and have a clear shot to the hoop. (Yes, I do think about these things while watching games.)

So brilliant me ... now that I have the "snake" under my belt and am officially responsible for making out the lineup for each game (thus more confidence) decides to offer a coaching suggestion to Coach Smith.

"Hey Jim", I say, "when playing 'D' our players along the baseline are consistently letting the ball handler drive right past them and directly to the hoop. They are not stopping baseline. Have you thought about coaching our boys to literally place one foot out of bounds along the baseline in an effort to cut off that baseline penetration?" Brilliant, right?

Coach Smith responded to me: "Is that legal?"

And of course, I said with great confidence: "Of course it is." (Who was I kidding?)

Why wouldn't it be I thought. Silly question I know.

So, at the next game Jim and I are conversing along the sidelines during a break in the action and one of the refs comes over. Jim looks over to him and describes what I had recommended regarding the baseline. (And as he is doing so I am praying "please be right…please be right".)

The ref looks at Jim and then looks at me and with a smile says:

"Oh, that is something you do not want to be teaching. By placing their foot out of bounds as soon as the defender makes contact with the ball it would be a turnover. They themselves will be out of bounds."

Darn it!

Jim thanked the ref and then looked at me, smiled, shook his head and walked away thinking:

"What an idiot, I can't believe he is an assistant coach for my team. What was I thinking? And I have him making out the line up too?" (As I said, I can read minds.)

Of course, from the time Jim walked away to the time of our next practice I am rationalizing in my head:

"Turnover? If we don't do something we will continue to give up easy layups by allowing baseline penetration. I will take the turnover if we stop the easy penetration and keep them outside."

But of course, no one was reading my mind. Oh well... I am not the head coach.

Time to step up and make a difference

As I assess the team I make note that as with most boys this age these boys do not "box out". Well, all except one.

Now how to get these boys who love to shoot and love to dribble to box out like the "Big Kid"?

It is time to go to "war".

From back when I was wearing out Google researching basketball drills and plays I recall finding a drill called "war".

War consists of 5 defensive players and 5 offensive players getting in basketball position (with the defense playing man-to-man). The Coach's role is to set the two teams up in good position, blow the whistle and call out "war" and then dribble, move, shoot and miss. (Great! I can do that really well).

The defensive team is to call out "shot!" as the shot is attempted to alert teammates to get in position and then immediately turn and box out their man. The offense's goal is to get around the box out and get the offensive rebound. The defense's job is to use the box out to get good position and get the defensive rebound.

Sounds easy right?

So, from the time of the infamous baseline error until the next practice I run this drill over and over in my head. And now it is Wednesday night and it is almost time for practice.

Tommy of course is yelling "Dad! We are going to be late."

I, of course, am spending much quality time in the bathroom. And then we are off to the practice.

On the way I tell Tommy about the drill and I can see that he is not getting it (meaning I am not explaining it well).

Uh oh…

Once we arrive at practice I take a deep breath or two while changing into my basketball sneakers and then seek out Jim.

"Jim, I have a drill I would like to use tonight that will improve our rebounding by improving our box out skills."

Jim begins to smile that big smile of his and responds, "If you can get the boys to call out 'shot' never mind boxing out I will be impressed".

Nothing like pressure.

Jim begins the practice. He sets the boys up in his standard layup drill. Make the layup … great. Miss the layup … push-ups. (More on that later.)

After layups Jim gives the boys a water break and then calls them to the center of the court. He informs the boys that Coach Dahlborg will be leading the next drill. Coach Dahlborg? Hope I don't have to say that.

I look at each boy and see in their eyes "Coach Dahlborg? Who? What does he know?" (Yup … still reading minds I am).

So yes, it is my turn to actually "coach". I take a breath and call the boys down to the far end of the court.

I tell the five starters that they are now on defense and playing man to man. I tell the other five boys to set up on offense. Once they are set up I explain this drill.

"We are going to play 'WAR'".

I ask, "Who knows how to box out? Who knows why we would want to box out?"

Tommy knows, and he explains.

That's my boy.

I thank Tommy and then further instruct each defender on how to box out and to yell "shot" when a shot is taken.

I explain why both of these things are important. Yes, the WHY. I also instruct the offensive players on how to beat the box out and get the offensive rebound and try to score on a "put back".

It is now time to run my first drill. I begin to dribble at the top of the key. I move right and then back to the left and put up a shot. It misses. (Surprised?)

No one yelled "shot". No one boxed out. 9 of 10 players went for the ball creating what looked like a Rugby scrum. Success? Well, not so much.

Time to regroup.

"Set it up! Set it up! Let's run it again. You all can do this. This is the type of thing that makes good players and good teams great. Let's go. When I put the ball up I want to hear all 5 defenders yell shot, box out and then attack the rebound. Let's go!"

We try again. I shoot. I miss. (No comment.)

I hear "shot". Not loud mind you but I do hear "shot" nonetheless. And I also see some of the defenders begin to try to box out. Success? A beginning. Our beginning.

"Set up! Set up! Let's run it again! This time if the team on defense gets the ball I want to see them run a fast break to the other end."

I shoot. I miss. I hear "shot". This time louder. Yes.

I see some more attempts at boxing out. The offensive team gets the rebound and puts a second shot up (a put back). No "Shot!" heard. No box out.

"Okay. Okay. We can do this. Each and every time a shot is attempted the defense should yell 'Shot!' very loud to alert teammates to box out. On the first shot. On the second shot. On each and every shot. Now let's get at it. I want to see the fast break! I want to see Magic!" (Pun intended)

Wow. Was I getting fired up? Was I getting loud? Is this coaching?

I shoot. I miss. I hear "SHOT!" loud. I see boxing out. I see the defensive team grab the rebound. I see them run a rudimentary fast break and hit an easy layup. *Magic to Worthy ... bang!*

"Nice! Very nice! See what can happen? Basics lead to points! Let's run it again!"

This is fun.

And so, it goes. Up and down the court we go. First with the starters on defense and then with the second team on defense. In fact, each team gets pretty good at it. Lots of shouting "Shot!" Lots of rebounds. Lots of fast breaks.

After about 15 minutes I tell the boys:

"Great job! Go get some water!" All the while thinking to myself "I experienced coaching. At least I think I did."

Shortly thereafter Jim shouts out the magic word … "SCRIMMAGE!" and the boys run and jump and yell and hustle to put on their pinnies (nylon mesh scrimmage jerseys) and get in position for a jump ball.

"This will be great" I think. "Now Jim will see that I can actually coach and make an impact".

I was feeling great as I walked to the sideline to stand with Coach Sampras (the calmest and coolest of the coaches … hmmmmm … would love for him to be my assistant coach … hmmmmm …).

So, the scrimmage begins and at first it is a little helter-skelter but then the boys set up their half-court offense and the defense gets in position. The offense dribbles, makes a pass, and takes the shot. "Shot!" I say to myself. "Box out!" I say to myself. Nope. No one yells shot. No one boxes out, except for one. Perhaps next time down the court. I wait. I watch. "Shot!" Nope. In fact, not once did anyone yell "Shot!" and not once did anyone box out, except one boy.

The scrimmage ends with lots of laughter and winded kids. Jim then pumps the team up for the next game and thanks me for my coaching.

I, of course, am thinking, "But it didn't translate to game conditions (or scrimmage conditions in this case). I didn't make a difference at all."

Chapter 9

Playing with a Girl?

Fast forward a few years ...

Haylee

Over the past couple of years my daughter Haylee and her good friend Sue would join us at Tommy's basketball practices pretty consistently. They would play on the stage, run around on the sidelines, and join in on some of the drills. Haylee eventually became our official ball girl (responsible for ensuring that our four good basketballs always arrived and came home with us at practices and games).

At the end of another admittedly draining basketball season (with me now as head coach) one evening after dinner my little Haylee said to me "Dad, do you want to go outside and shoot hoops?"

At first, I thought she was kidding as she had never asked to "shoot hoops" before. But once realizing she was serious I said "sure, let's play". We then went out front to our basketball hoop (where Tommy and I had worked on "boxing out" years prior).

We begin with me with the ball feeding passes to Haylee and lo and behold she is hitting every shot, i.e., inside shots, outside jump-shots, layups. She is hitting them all. She then takes another pass, pivots, fakes, and drives and scores again. My gosh...when did she learn how to play?

"Haylee, you are amazing! When did you get so good?"

"Dad, I have been practicing with Tommy's team for years."

Oh my. What a great father I am. I always made sure Haylee was safe during practices and that she had fun and had opportunities to participate but truth be told I never really focused on her game.

And here we are in front of our house and … She can shoot. She can pass. She can pivot, and she can move, and she can drive. She is great!

"You are great, Haylee. Thank you for playing with me tonight."

"Thank you for playing with me, Daddy."

When I got inside I shared with Doc what had just happened and how good Haylee is. We were both amazed. Haylee has always been our "baby", our "angel", our "porcelain doll". Is she these things and a powerful talented athlete? Both And?

I decided to not press basketball with Haylee but rather to let her decide when or if she wanted to "shoot hoops" again. I was just thrilled she asked me once to play and seemed to enjoy it and did not want to put any pressure on her.

The next night after dinner my little Haylee said again, "Daddy, do you want to shoot hoops with me?"

Yes! I thought. "Sure Haylee. I would love to."

And we were at it again and she was just as good the second time. And then over time the third time, the fourth time and so on.

"Do you think you might want to play for the school team?"

"Daddy, there is no 6th grade school team. I want to play rec ball with you as my coach!"

Oh my god. Learning how to coach boys is still very challenging. How do you coach a group of girls? Is it different than coaching boys?

"I love you Haylee. You are an amazing basketball player. Do you really enjoy it?"

"I love basketball, Daddy!"

Towards the end of the summer Coach Sampras, his son Dean, Tommy and I decided we would begin to play basketball on the Gorham Middle School outdoor courts on Sunday mornings (when the weather allows).

"Haylee, would you like to play with us on Sunday mornings?"

"Oh yeah!"

"Are you sure? Will she get hurt?" Doc asked me after I had already extended the invite.

"She will be fine. She is really good and besides … Tommy will always protect her."

On Facebook:

Me:

"Pete [Coach Sampras] 9am Sunday hoops?"

Pete:

"Sounds great Tom. We (Pete and Dean) will be there."

Me:

"Awesome! This will be great!"

"Haylee is going to play too. Watch out for her. She is really good."

I am guessing Pete was thinking I was just being nice … little did he know.

The Game

"First two to hit are on a team!" We shot free throws to make teams just like back in my Old Colony Y (YMCA) days in Brockton.

"Okay Haylee. Your shot."

SWISHHHH!!

"Great shot Haylee!" Pete said.

"I told you Pete. Watch out."

"Wow. She is good."

Eventually it was my shot and no swish, but I did hit it.

"Haylee – you and me!"

I love watching my children smile those big smiles that truly show the joy and happiness coming from their heart. That is what Haylee shared with me this day.

"Yay Daddy! Let's beat them."

Okay. Easier said than done. It will be Haylee (clearly a phenom) and me against Tommy who is now a great shooter (especially three pointers), Dean (no one rebounds better), and Pete (who is about 280 and very strong and owns the inside).

"Okay. Let's shoot for outs!" Time to shoot three pointers to decide which team will have the ball first.

BANG!

Yup. Tommy hit the three-pointer. Their ball.

"Haylee, we will play zone. You cover the outside and I will cover the inside."

"Okay, daddy."

"You better cover her Pete when we have the ball. She is really good."

As Pete runs by me to get in position he says "I know. I know."

I don't think he knows.

Dean passes the ball in to Tommy. Haylee slides over to cover Tommy on the outside. (Note: a good zone defense should not look too dissimilar from a helping man-to-man defense). I am about 7 feet from the hoop in position to pick Tommy up if he moves inside, while also looking to defend a cross-pass to

Dean and trying not to let Pete get good position underneath on me.

Tommy dribbles and shoots and misses. I grab the rebound and dribble out to the clear line (we are using the three-point line to clear the ball on every possession change).

Dean and Tommy come out to defend me. Pete remains underneath for rebounds. I dribble right and drive between the two defenders until I arrive at Pete. I pass the ball behind my back to Haylee wide-open about 10 feet from the hoop.

"Shoot Haylee!"

SWISHHH!

"You have got to cover her Pete."

"I know. I know."

Now he knows.

Their ball. Dean passes the ball in to Pete. Pete drives hard to the hoop. He sees Haylee and me both dropping down to stop him. He stops and hits Tommy in the corner. BANG!

"That's a three-pointer, Tommy. Nice shot!"

"Thanks, Dad."

"Our ball Haylee. Do you want to pass it in or do you want me to do it?"

"I'll pass it in Daddy," she says with a huge smile.

I lean into Dean and then break away toward Haylee. She hits me at the top of the key. She runs to her spot. I see Pete slide over to cover her.

He learns quickly.

I drive hard to the right around Dean. Haylee does a V-cut toward the hoop and then back to her spot. I am slightly stunned but have enough time to get her the ball just as she turns to me.

She shoots (without even being told).

SWISHHH! 4 to 3 we are winning. "Great shot Haylee!" Pete yells.

Haylee smiles that big beautiful smile of hers.

"Haylee...where did you learn to do a V-cut?"

"Oh Daddy, I learned that at your practices."

My gosh, was I blind. She learned so much and I missed it. Great father I am. Great coach I am.

Tommy passes the ball in to Pete. Haylee covers the outside man, Dean. Pete lowers his shoulder and like a Mack Truck drives toward the hoop. I slide away from Tommy and into the path of the Mack Truck. Boom! Shoulder into my chest. I fall back. Pete takes a shot from 2 feet. He misses. I am recovering to get back in the play. Pete gets his own rebound, shoots again and scores.

5 to 4 we are losing.

"Let's get 'em Haylee," I say with a smile.

"Okay Daddy!" She smiles back.

I pass the ball in to Haylee. She drives with her right hand to the right side of the court. Pete and Tommy close on her. She then crosses-over and drives with her left hand to the other side of the court.

"Haylee can cross-over dribble?" I say to myself. "Haylee can dribble with little effort with her opposite hand?" I continue. "Where have I been?"

Her move is phenomenal and provides her with just enough space to get off her third shot.

SWISHHH! 6 to 5 we are winning. "Wow Haylee!" Tommy screams.

"Haylee", I begin, "a cross-over move and then dribbling with your left hand? That is great!"

"Thank you, Daddy. You taught us at Tommy's practices."

How should I feel? I taught "us". I was doing my best to teach the boys. I had no idea I was teaching my little angel.

The game continues. Dean passes over to Tommy. Pete boxes me out. Haylee slide steps in front of Tommy. Tommy drives past her on the baseline to the hoop. (I hate when baseline is given up). I come over to cover him. Tommy jumps and manipulates his body so that his lower body is facing the baseline and his shoulders, arms and head are facing the rim.

SWISHHH! 7 to 6 they are now winning. "Great move!" I call out to Tommy. "How did you twist like that?"

"I have been working on my core downstairs three days a week."

"Wow. Your hard work is really paying off" I tell him.

The game goes back and forth with Haylee scoring ten of our 18 points. For the other team Tommy has scored 7, Pete 4 and Dean 6. We are at 18 to 17. A three-pointer for them will win it. They have the ball.

"Okay Haylee," I whisper. "We cannot give up a three. You will need to stay in front of Tommy and not let him get a three-point shot off. Don't give him a good look. We can live with a two but not a three."

"Okay Daddy."

I hug Haylee and then position myself so that it looks like I will cover Tommy. Dean is passing the ball in.

I notice Pete cuts away from the hoop toward the three-point line half-way to the corner.

"Uh oh!" I yell. "Screen!"

Pete has set a screen for Tommy. Both Haylee and I are screened for a brief moment. Dean fires the ball like Pedro Martinez throwing his two-seam fastball towards Tommy (who has run through the screen perfectly ensuring no room between him and Pete so that I cannot fight through) and is now wide-open in the corner for his patented three-pointer to win it. At the last second, I get my hand up and the ball deflects off of my pinkie just past Tommy and out of bounds.

"Great play! Great pass!" I say to the other team while gasping for air as I walk off the court (very slowly while taking deep breaths) to retrieve the ball.

"Haylee. They almost had us on that one. We need to be looking for the screen."

"No worries Daddy. We got this one!"

How my little girl has grown up.

Their ball again. This time Pete is passing the ball in. Dean stays up top past the three-point line. This time Tommy drops deep into the corner. Clearly, they are spreading us out.

I whisper to Haylee, "I will take Tommy man-to-man this time. Stay up tight on Dean. If they get the two that is still okay."

Pete looks for Tommy in the corner, but I am there. Tommy starts to move toward Pete while continuing to remain behind the three-point line.

Dean breaks for the hoop and Pete throws him the ball just over the reach of Haylee. Dean puts it up off the backboard, but it has a little too much force and bounces off the rim and away. I had run to box out Pete as I saw him crashing the boards. We collide with the Mack Truck again winning the battle against this Prius. The ball bounces past the three of us back to Haylee at the foul line. Haylee grabs it and just as she spins toward the clear-line Tommy charges in and knocks the ball away. Dean beats me to the ball while Tommy has repositioned himself in the corner. Dean makes a two-handed pass out to Tommy who is now wide open again for the three.

Tommy receives the ball as Haylee is running over to him. With her hands up and near his face he shoots one of those "Robert Parish-esque" rainbow shots. And as in slow motion we all turn and watch the ball leave Tommy's fingers, ascend into the air with a slight backspin, pass in front of the sun like a magical eclipse, continue to travel through the blue sky, and then begin its descent slowly toward the hoop.

While this is happening, I am thinking how much I love my son. How he has grown and matured in his game. How he is such a tremendous shooter. And how I really want him to miss this one time. (Don't tell him I said that.)

The ball appears to actually hit inside the hoop the way you see on TV when a pro makes that perfect shot and the net actually pops, but somehow this time it is different. At what appears to be the very last second the ball jumps back up, hits the side of the rim, then the other, and then seems to be pulled straight up and out of the hoop and away to the far side of the court.

We all continue to look at the rim and then finally at the ball and watch as it rolls out of bounds.

Amazing. Perhaps this is Haylee's chance for her win?

"That was incredible Tommy. Great setup. Great release. Great shot. Thought you had us. Wow."

"Thanks Dad. I thought I had it too."

As I go and get the ball (again very slowly as I try to catch my breath) I tell Haylee that her sliding over to pick up Tommy made just enough of a difference on that play. "Nice job." I say.

Okay. Still 18 to 17. Our ball. I am tired. We need to win soon.

"What do you want to do Haylee?"

"I want to shoot." She says with confidence. Just like her Pa (my Dad).

"Okay. You inbound the ball to me and then get open in your spot."

"Okay Daddy."

Pete sets up down low. Dean is defending the inbounds pass. Tommy is fronting me daring Haylee to try to pass the ball past the Condor-arms of Dean and over Tommy's head.

Remembering Haylee's V-cut from earlier, I cut down to the post and use Pete as a screen to get a step on Tommy. Haylee fakes a pass to an imaginary player to her right as I come up on her left. Dean goes for the fake which gives Haylee a split-second to make a solid bounce pass to me. I grab it and pivot hard to the hoop.

Both Dean and Tommy close in on me…

Haven't they learned? Don't they know who the real athlete is on this team?

…as Haylee runs to her spot.

Pete reverses and tries to slide up to cover Haylee.

He has learned.

I look to Haylee and then split the double-team and drive to the hoop with both Dean and Tommy chasing me. Pete sees me driving and leaves Haylee to stop the penetration. "Perfect!" I think "Haylee will be wide open." But then out of the corner of my eye I see Dean and Tommy (who both must have been thinking the same as me) leave my trail to go and double Haylee.

"Uh oh!" flashes through my mind until I see Haylee fake a quick V-cut to the far corner and then double-back around her two pursuers and against their momentum so that she is now trailing me. I immediately give an up-fake to Pete, leave an over-the-head drop-pass for Haylee and circle around to box Pete out for any rebound. Haylee grabs and shoots the ball in one quick motion (Ray Allen anyone?) just as Dean and Tommy reach her.

The ball goes up just over the fingertips of Dean. The ball hits the backboard and goes through the hoop. A perfect Sam Jones bank shot.

We win!

"Haylee you did it!" I yell.

"Haylee! Great shot!" Pete says.

Tommy and Dean in unison say, "That was great Haylee! 20 to 17. You win. Great game."

"Thanks Mr. Sampras. Great game Tommy. Great game Dean." she says.

"What a game Haylee! You scored 12 of our points! You got the winning basket! You rock!" I am so happy for her.

"Thank you, Daddy. You played great too."

Awwwwww … "Thanks Haylee."

"Let's shoot for teams for the next game." And off we went…

Most Sunday mornings (weather permitting) the five of us (sometimes more) would get together at the Gorham Middle School to play basketball. And each Sunday Tommy, Dean and Haylee would get better and better. Pete would too, especially on the inside. Me? I judged my efforts by how much ice I needed on my knees each afternoon. The more ice, the harder I played, the better I felt. Yes, I know. Doc says a little crazy.

More importantly though I was witnessing these children coming together to play, to learn, to grow, to have fun, to support one another, and doing so because they truly love to do so. Doing so because they truly love.

Remember when I said, "does life get any better?" It just did. God truly blesses.

Chapter 10

Letting My Daughter Down

As Fall approached Haylee was talking about basketball more and more. Her passion and excitement for the game increased exponentially since first asking me to play with her; and her anticipation of playing 6th grade girls Gorham recreational basketball was palpable.

"Daddy, will you coach me in recreational basketball?"

Oh my. I am drained. The boys season still fresh in my mind. The infamous "you are the worst coach ever" E-mail still etched in my cerebral cortex.

I reflected on what a wonderful physician friend of mine had shared about the differences in coaching girls and boys, "Girls have a passion for being together and a willingness to play as a team; they focus more so on the game and less so on the score."

I also recalled the movie "The Heart of the Game" about an unorthodox girls' basketball coach in Seattle who had nurtured an amazing program. From the movie's tagline: "THE HEART OF THE GAME captures the passion and energy of a Seattle high school girls' basketball team, the eccentricity of their unorthodox coach."

I love my daughter. I love playing basketball (and other sports) with her.

[NOTE: My favorite thing to do with my daughters is watching them both perform in their dance recitals (but that is for another time).]

I don't know if I am capable of coaching a girls' team.

Am I eccentric (like the Seattle coach)? Perhaps.

Do I have unorthodox coaching philosophies and is my style of coaching different than my peers? Absolutely. (I've been told.)

As I am continuing to learn how to coach a boys' team and striving to position each of these boys for success on and off the court am I truly what my daughter and this girls' team really need (especially when there are experienced coaches available)?

Serendipitously (and literally) the next day I received an E-mail from the same individual who informed me that I was the worst coach ever.

As I saw the subject of the E-mail "Coaching" and who it is from (Brian Boxswain) I was taken aback and thought:

"Well, Haylee's request has been answered. Knowing Brian believes me to be the worst coach ever this must be a sign from God that I am not supposed to coach Haylee's rec team."

And then I opened the E-mail.

> DEAR TOM,
>
> IT APPEARS HAYLEE AND SUE (this fellow's daughter who attended Tommy's practices with Haylee on many occasions) WILL BE PLAYING REC BASKETBALL ON THE SAME TEAM. I INTEND TO COACH BUT WILL BE TRAVELING A LOT. WOULD YOU BE INTERESTED IN COACHING WITH ME? I BELIEVE IT WOULD BE FUN TO COACH TOGETHER.
>
> JUST LET ME KNOW.
>
> BRIAN

Huh? (I clearly still have my way with words.) What am I supposed to do with this? Is this a bad joke? He said I was the worst coach ever. I don't understand.

I still have the open wounds from the previous E-mail. Just seeing the subject of this E-mail made my gut hollow out. I don't want to disappoint my daughter, but I cannot coach with this individual. Not after what he wrote. Not now understanding what he 'truly' thinks of me.

In sharing this E-mail with my bride, she knew exactly what to say (as always).

"Why do you always do this to yourself? What you read in that original E-mail and what that original E-mail said were not the same thing. And I know for a fact Brian thinks you are a great coach. Besides, would he have asked you to coach with him if he didn't respect you as a coach?"

Doc shared more that evening and logically I knew her to be right (she always is ... but don't tell her I said so) and yet ...

And yet even with this new wisdom (shared with both care and love) I was not ready to coach a second team. (At least I convinced myself that this was a truth. My truth.)

"Haylee, I love you. It appears Mr. Boxswain has been selected to coach your team. He has asked me to coach with him. But...

(as I held back tears) ...

... this year I would love to continue to play basketball with you on Sundays, have you continue to join Tommy's practices (our practices) [and to myself I made note to ensure I am far more mindful of Haylee's play during these practices], and also for me to attend all of your games as a spectator so that I can thoroughly enjoy watching you play the game you love."

Gulp.

"I hope you understand."

"Oh, Daddy, I love playing with you and Tommy. I would love you to coach me but of course I understand. You can coach me on the weekends. Mr. Boxswain can coach me during the week."

Yup … roll tears.

Why are my children so much more mature than me?

I am so blessed and so grateful to God for all three of my children. I am so humbled each and every day and inspired by all three of them to grow, mature, and to be better than I really am.

I am also quite impacted by how I am letting my daughter down.

Chapter 11

Chest Day!

So how did we go from "the worst coach ever" to being requested to coach by both my daughter (most importantly) and by the author of the infamous E-mail?

Perhaps it began with ... for those who tend to hit the weights ... "chest day!"

Or something like that.

At the beginning of my second season assisting Coach Smith I made a mental note of something I respectfully disagreed with in his coaching repertoire. (Again, noting that Jim is an excellent coach.)

During practices, one of the drills he would lead is to have the boys split up into two lines. Each line at half court, each line also along the sideline, and each line facing the opposite basket. Each child has a basketball and at the sound of the whistle each child one by one runs and dribbles toward the hoop in front of them, shoots a short jump shot, gets their own rebound and then runs while dribbling to get in the back of the other line until it's their turn to go again this time at the opposite hoop.

Well, that is the typical approach.

Coach Smith added a twist to this. He believed it would be beneficial to provide an opportunity for these boys to also get physically stronger as part of this drill. So, when a child missed their shot he would instruct them to hit the floor and complete 10 push-ups. (Yes, chest day! ... or at least that is what I would have said back in 1987 when I was hitting the gym 7 days a week and it was "chest day!" Monday, Tuesday, Wednesday, Thursday, Friday, Saturday, and Sunday. (So much for smart training ... said with my Boston accent.))

But in the scenario above I struggled with this concept. Noting that at first, I did not understand why I was struggling and second, I was not sure what to do with this struggle.

So, as an extreme introvert (an 'I' in the Myers-Briggs framework) I processed this struggle. A lot.

Why does this seemingly innocuous addition to a standard drill bother me?

– Coach Smith has the best intentions.

– The boys are getting stronger.

– I love chest day. (At least I did.)

So why is this bothering me and what am I going to do with this information?

So, as the season kicked off at practice each week we would run this drill. And as with most teams the boys missed more shots than they made and thus they were hitting the floor and doing many many push-ups.

And I continued to be nagged by the feeling that "this is not right"; along with the "what do I know?"; "who am I to second guess Coach Smith?"; "I should just keep my mouth shut and do my little part"; "it's not a big deal anyway".

But then it hit me.

It was not about push-ups. It was not about getting the boys stronger. My concern was about how do we best position these boys to improve their shooting. Yes, repetition is important and yet as Michael Jordan noted …

> *"You can practice shooting eight hours a day, but if your technique is wrong, then all you become is very good at shooting the wrong way."*

And was the boys' technique wrong … yes. But they are still quite young and still learning under the tutelage of Coach Smith, Coaches Wright and Sampras, and under me, the physical aspects of technique.

What I had been struggling with was the mental aspect of the game. And quite frankly, what I had witnessed was the fact that during this drill many of the boys were beginning to focus more on the push-ups (and not wanting to do them) then on taking a quality shot with proper technique. Their EQ (emotional quotient) ... or in other words their ability to control their emotion regardless of changing circumstances ... had not developed yet as their focus went from practicing "J's" (jump shots) to seeking to avoid push-ups. And because of this (based on my rudimentary analysis of shots made ... done without the benefits of an excel spreadsheet this time) their shooting percentage was actually going down.

There it is. After three weeks of processing (they say we "I's" live in our head a great deal ... and I tend to do so more than others according to reliable sources ... yes, my bride being one of them) I arrived at what was triggering me and now it was time to determine what I was going to do with this information.

On one hand, we have a great coach (Coach Smith) leading a team of young men who are having fun, exercising, learning a sport, playing a game they love, and doing so as they learn how to become a team. And on the other hand, as an assistant coach isn't it my responsibility to bring concerns I make note of to the head coach and to discuss as adults these differing philosophies? And wouldn't I be shirking my responsibility if I did not?

The week between the practice when it all came together for me and the following practice I decided that yes it was indeed my responsibility to share my concern with Coach Smith (with Jim). And for those 6 days I ran the conversation through my mind over and over and over. (Of course, based on my history the scenarios usually did not play out well. Either Jim totally dismissed my feedback (and thus me) or he actually became angry for his philosophy and process being questioned by a rookie (a second-year volunteer assistant coach)).

Ugh.

So here we go again …

Okay, it is the evening of the next practice which begins at 7:00pm at the Village School.

I can feel my nerves. The pit of my stomach is both hollow and enlarged at the same time and grumbling nonstop.

Tommy on the other hand is pumped and ready to go as always. The lion is ready to roar again.

"Come on dad…we are going to be late."

It is 6:30pm.

"Let's go dad!"

It takes less than 5 minutes to get there.

"Dad, where are you? Come on … I don't want to be late! Come on!"

Okay, we are eventually in the car and on our way to practice. Tommy pumped and ready to practice. Me dreading the conversation I am about to have.

We arrive, and I head to the men's room as always as Tommy heads to the gym.

By the time Tommy has changed his sneakers and is shooting around with the other boys prior to practice, I have arrived in the gym and locate Coach Smith. He is as always full of energy, running, jumping, shooting, and laughing with the boys.

"Jim!" I say forcefully with my deep rich James Earl Jones voice.

Actually … I say "JIM" with what sounds more like Barney Fife yelling for Andy Taylor … as I walk not-so-confidently toward him.

"Hey Tom!" Jim says with great vigor and joy.

"Jim, I wanted to talk to you prior to the start of practice."

"Of course, what's up?"

"I have a concern. A … um … c-concern with something we are having the boys do in practice."

"Really?!?! What do you know and who are you to say anything. Go sit on the sideline and continue to humiliate yourself with "great" suggestions like that "step out of bounds to stop baseline" recommendation. Pathetic!"

Okay … that is what was said in my head.

This is what really happened after I expressed my concern and recommendation. (Which was essentially let's separate the strength building from the shooting drill so that the boys can focus more on the physical technique of shooting during the shooting drill and no longer worry about push-ups as a penalty of missing. Thus, freeing their minds a bit. The strength training would be done separately as it is still very important.)

And Jim's response …

"Tom, I see what you are saying. Let's make the change starting today."

No big deal. No offense taken. No ego. Just "let's make the change".

And so, we did.

Coach Smith has taught me much about coaching. And he has done so in the best possible way … in action. I learned that day (and many days after) how to coach from Jim. I also learned in many ways how to be a better teammate, employee, leader, father, husband and member of the community.

I have never told Jim what his tutelage of me has meant to me and how it has impacted not only me but many others that I have been blessed to serve.

Perhaps I should.

Chapter 12

Body Image

Building a Team

By the time Tommy was in 8th grade I had become the head
coach for this middle school rec basketball team with Pete
Sampras and Doug Norgaard (another boy's father) as my two
volunteer assistant coaches.

As mentioned previously, I had learned a great deal from
Coach Smith and was now leveraging and evolving this
learning in an effort to position all of these boys (and girls in
the case of Haylee who continues to join our practices and
now has become team manager, ball girl, and emergency
scoreboard keeper when needed) to learn and grow.

Assessments

Each year, prior to the season, we have an assessment of all the children interested in playing rec basketball in Gorham. The assessment includes all the boys running drills and scrimmaging while the coaches of each of the Gorham rec teams watch and assess each child to determine who they want on their team. (Unlike a draft every child who wants play makes a team).

Tommy, continuing his passion for the game, was aching to be on the court for the assessment.

"Come on, Dad. We are going to be late!"

"The assessment is at 8:00am. It's only 6:30am."

"But Dad, I want to warm up."

Well, you know the rest.

So, we arrive on time and I make my usual trek to the men's room prior to joining the assessment process.

At the beginning of the assessment, each head coach is handed a worksheet with each child's name, contact information, and the number they will be wearing (for easier identification).

The Gorham Rec Director explains the "how to's" to us coaches and then calls all the boys together and explains the drills to each of them as well.

Then the whistle blows, and the boys are off. First running a "weave" and then layups, passing, short jumpers, and lastly two simultaneous scrimmages (to ensure each child has the opportunity to play under game conditions and be assessed).

As this is going on I (being the introvert and living mostly in my head) walk away from all the other coaches and begin a slow circle of the gym. As I am walking I am seeking players who I want on my team. Who is hustling? Who is following directions? Who is "finding the open man" and playing as part of a team during the scrimmage? Who is boxing out and rebounding? (Well ... I know at least one boy who is). Who is hustling on both ends of the court? Who is finding joy in the game? Yes, pure God-given talent stands out for sure. And yes, there was some of that displayed. And yet, I sought out boys that I believed I could also help. And as I circled and watched I made notations as to who I wanted on my team and when (which round) I hoped to select that boy for the team.

Soon the scrimmages are over, and the Rec Director explains to the boys the rest of the process and dismisses them. He then calls us coaches into a room set up with a number of tables and chairs for us to "draft" (to select) our team. Because Tommy is my son and Coach Sampras and Coach Norgaard also have sons wanting to play, my team already had these three players automatically assigned to it. Other Coaches also had sons playing but at this time no more than two, so my team had the last selection in each round.

The other coaches selected very talented players with their first couple of picks. And yet I was thrilled that the boys I had prioritized for my team were still "on the board" (as they say during the NFL draft ... or perhaps during your Fantasy Football team draft). And over the next 45 minutes or so our team was created.

The team was comprised of ... HEART. Each boy I selected was selected because I saw their heart either on the court or in brief discussions, or previously during the baseball season or other. Some were extremely talented. Some were there because they wanted to play on a team. All had heart.

That evening I sent out an email to all the players and their parents letting them know that they were selected to be on this team and let them know who their teammates were, who their coaches were, contact information, when and where we will have practices, when games will be played, and also at a high-level my coaching philosophy and expectations for the players and families.

And this was the beginning of me (as a head coach) coaching my son and his friends and doing so with two dedicated, caring fathers volunteering as assistant coaches (and of course Haylee as team manager).

Assumptions

Going into a new season (and especially as a new head coach) I made many assumptions. Many spot-on ... one in particular way off.

Our team continued to practice at the Village School (an older small gym with bright fluorescent lights and slippery floors). And on some occasions pinnies were not available at this location.

So, as I planned for the first practice of this new season I made sure I wrote and rehearsed an initial short speech for the team (learning from my first practice as an assistant coach that just saying my name accurately and with confidence is quite important) …

"Bring it in! Hold on to the basketballs. There is no dribbling when I say, 'bring it in!' nor when any of us three coaches are speaking.

I am Coach Dahlborg. This is Coach Sampras and Coach Norgaard. And this is your team. This is OUR team. Let's go around and introduce ourselves. Tommy please start … (it is tough to be the coach's son) …

I said this is our TEAM. By definition, we are a team. But we have much work to do to truly live up to that word. I selected each of you for this team for specific reasons. I expect much and the bar is high. We are here to support one another and do our best to help each of us get better and succeed. And if we each succeed the team succeeds and we are successful.

We will learn together. We will grow together. We will get better together. We will exercise together, and we will have fun.

Are we ready to play basketball?!?!"

"YES!"

"Let's go! Two lines!"

(Layup drill)

I also developed new and (hopefully) interesting drills and plays meant to both teach and help to improve the game of each of these boys. And from day one, with much help from Coaches Sampras and Norgaard, we instituted these drills and plays.

Back to the assumption

As I mentioned, at the Village School pinnies were not always available and at this time our team did not have those cool reversible jerseys where one side was white and the other a color to make it easy to split up into two teams to scrimmage.

"You boys are on the white team … You boys are on the blue team. Flip your jerseys and let's go."

No. We did not have these jerseys … yet. And with pinnies being in question … I made assumptions prior to our first practice.

I reviewed my roster and identified (based on my assumptions) which children might have a concern with playing "shirts versus skins".

[Shirts vs Skins – means one group of boys is wearing their t-shirts and the other group of boys is not wearing a jersey (done so that during the heat of action of a scrimmage each team can easily see who is on their own team and who is not)].

Knowing Tommy (and having discussed with him prior) I knew he would be uncomfortable at this age playing on the 'skins' team. I then looked at the rest of the roster and made assumptions. Who else would more likely be uncomfortable playing without a jersey? And after much thought I made a list. If the pinnies are not available for our practice I will divide the team up this way for the scrimmage.

So along with my short speech, philosophy, rules, roster, and the list of drills and plays I had developed, I also documented and placed in my back pocket the list of boys who will be on the 'shirts' team and the boys who will be on the 'skins' team … just in case.

So, here we go again …

Okay, it is the evening of our first practice which begins at 7:00pm at the Village School.

Tommy is pumped and ready to go as always. So am I … even as I feel my nerves and the hollow of my enlarged grumbling gut.

"Come on dad…we are going to be late."

It is 6:30pm.

"Let's go dad!"

It takes less than 5 minutes to get there.

"Dad, where are you? Come on ... I don't want to be late! Come on!"

God, I love his passion and enthusiasm!

We arrive at the Village School and after my usual stop in the men's room I seek out coaches Sampras and Norgaard and thank them for coaching with me ... and then begin the search for the elusive pinnies.

Lo and behold there are no pinnies to be found.

We have a solid first practice and as we get to the 15-minute mark left in practice I blow my whistle and yell "who wants to scrimmage?!"

Have you ever seen sharks "smell" blood in the water (I am not sure if sharks actually smell ... will need to ask my daughter Sammy (the shark expert)) and they go into a frenzy around whatever was bleeding? Well ... that doesn't compare to eighth grade boys hearing that magic word "SCRIMMAGE!" They came from everywhere. Those on the court already ... came running, jumping, yelling, smiling. Those at the water bubbler did 180's and sprinted to midcourt. Even those in the boys' bathroom came running (hopefully after washing their hands first).

"Okay boys. This is our first scrimmage. We will be playing shirts verses skins. Those on the 'shirts' team are Tommy, ____, ____, ____ and those on the 'skins' team will be ____, ____, ____, ____."

Body Image

Despite public perception, body image issues and eating disorders are not exclusively female problems. The oft-cited figure is that about 1 in 10 eating disorders occur in males, but latest research shows this number to be closer to 1 in 4. Male or female the issues with body image is a challenge we need to first be aware of and second determine how best to manage.

In this case, my assumption was wrong.

As soon as I said the name of one particular boy he immediately yelled, "No! I will not be on the 'skins' team!" and ran out of the gymnasium.

My criteria to determine who I believed would be least likely to have a body image issue was wrong. I screwed up. And I screwed up big. Thank God Coach Sampras (who was close to this young man) was there.

As I focused on the other 11 players (focused is a tough word because my heart was out the door with Coach Sampras and this boy) ... Pete sat with this boy, talked with this boy, and encouraged him to return to practice.

When this boy came back into the gymnasium I handed over the rest of the team to Coaches Norgaard and Sampras and then I sat with this boy and (as I had learned from Coach Smith's demeanor when I raised an issue with him) softly and calmly let this boy know that I had made a mistake, I was sorry, and that he indeed was on the 'shirts' team.

To my astonishment this boy immediately jumped up and ran over to the 'shirts' team and proceeded to dominate the scrimmage with his jumping, rebounding, blocking shots, and hustle (all the reasons I wanted him on this team in the first place).

Body Image Issues are a Big Deal

Studies have found that the desire to bulk up by boys with body image issues was linked to future abuse of drugs, alcohol, muscle-enhancing supplements and steroids. And those boys seeking to be thinner were more likely to develop depression.

I screwed up, and in doing so I adversely impacted a child … and I learned.

As a coach these are the MOST important things …

- Being aware of these issues (check),

- Developing authentic relationships with players and families so that challenging conversations can take place with honesty and while balancing heart and mind (I believe we ended up getting there),

- Talking with your team proactively about issues such as this (BIG missed opportunity),

- With your team or the individual or (if appropriate) the family determining how best to manage (check but only after initial mistake),

- and NEVER making these types of assumptions,

… again, these are the things that are most important. These are the things coaches of boys and girls must understand (yes, even more so than the X's and O's).

Perhaps the lesson I learned about assumptions and body image will serve to help another coach.

I hope so.

Chapter 13

Superman

Early practices for a new team (including a first-year head coach) involve many tests.

Tests of players by coaches. And tests of coaches by players. Or at least one would think so.

Early on it was apparent … we were a team.

Yes, we would test and grow and learn. But mostly we would learn. Together as a team. A very special team. We would learn.

Chest Passes

"Chest passes! Set up two lines. Today we are going to learn how to get the ball safely from you to your target (the closest open player). Who knows what 'safely' means when we talk about passing a ball safely?"

"Okay. Tommy. What do I mean be 'safely'?"

"Safely means the ball does not get stolen by the other team."

"That's right, Tommy. We work way too hard to get possession of the ball to then turnaround and hand the ball right back over to the other team with an ill-advised or poorly executed pass. Once we have possession of the ball we want to keep it until ideally the ball goes through the net."

"I want each player in the line closest to me to have a basketball.

Now …

- If you are right-handed place your right hand on top of the ball and your left hand to the side.

- Bring the ball to chest level.

- Grip the ball with your fingertips and have your fingers evenly spread with your elbows tucked into your body.

- When you go to pass the ball take a step in the direction of the target being sure to keep your other foot in pivot position, so you do not get called for 'traveling'.

- Use your 'pivot foot' to push off and generate power behind your pass.

- Generally, a good chest pass is delivered by stepping with your dominant foot. If you're right-handed, you'll usually step forward with your right foot. However, it's important to be able to deliver a clean chest pass by stepping forward with either foot.

- Extend your arms fully and push the ball in a straight line toward the chest of the closest open man.

- Be sure to follow through by thrusting your arms and snapping your wrists. Your hands will end up with your pinkies pointing upward and your thumbs pointing downward.

- The backs of your hands should be facing each other.

… got it?"

"Yes, coach!" I hear Jimmy yell. God, I love this kid's enthusiasm.

Unfortunately, most of the other players with the ball in their hands look a bit bewildered and the ones ready to receive the ball just as puzzled.

"That's great, Jimmy. And boys, there are NO worries. I just shared a lot of information. This is practice. We are practicing. We are practicing together. Don't worry if you don't get it at first. You will and coaches Norgaard, Sampras and I will help."

Yes. We are a team.

For the next 20 minutes the players made chest passes back and forth.

From Jimmy to Tommy and from Tommy back to Jimmy.

From Jon to David and then back to Jon.

From Haylee to Michael and then back to Haylee.

And so on and so on ... over and over and over.

According to Navy Seal lore, "under pressure you don't rise to the occasion, you sink to the level of your training". Although this is "only" recreation basketball as coaches it is our responsibility to ensure the children are well trained to achieve their goals on the court (and off the court which we will find out later).

Each pair of players made chest passes with us three coaches reminding, showing, instructing, teaching, coaching and recognizing as they raised their level of play.

And together we learned how to make a chest pass.

"Great work, team. Now go get some water."

Superman

I had initially noticed Jimmy during the player assessment a few weeks back. Brown shaggy hair. Brown eyes. Of average height. A little slumped over in his walk. A boy who rarely made eye contact. Always chomping on gum.

On the sidelines and in-between drills, he simply looked like another player desiring to play the game of basketball for hopefully the right reasons.

And yet … he was not just "another player" which I saw as I stood alone and watched the assessment scrimmages.

NOTE: And based on Jimmy being available for me to select late in the draft (due to my team's low draft position) apparently, I was the only coach blessed to see this boy's gift at this time.

Scrimmage

Jason, one of the more talented ball players being assessed has the ball under his own hoop. He dribbles left as he runs toward half court. There are two of his teammates open ahead. One at the elbow where a nice back door lob pass would lead to an easy bucket and another a foot behind the arc all set to bury a three.

Jason is not looking up but rather focusing his attention on the two defenders in front of him. He crossover dribbles from left to right as he approaches the defenders and then using his athleticism and his good ball handling skills he stops on a dime and takes two intentional steps backward in an effort to gap the double team.

Unfortunately, while Jason is focusing on the two defenders in front of him and preparing to make his next move a third defender comes up from behind him and 'picks his pocket' by timing Jason's next crossover dribble and with his palm facing up knocking the ball forward to one of the double teamers.

"No 'reaching in' foul", I think. "Simply great hustle, an excellent move, and solid team defense."

With this, the boy who has received the ball takes off toward the hoop with his partners in crime (or at least partners in stealing basketballs during an assessment scrimmage) filling the lanes (providing passing options to the new ball handler). Jason, clearly a bit frustrated turns and watches as the triad drives to the hole for an easy bucket.

A three on none (three offensive players with the ball and no defense in sight).

Or at least I thought so as literally out of nowhere a streak of grey flies by me as I stand on the sideline parallel to the foul line on the near side of the court.

The boy who had made the initial steal has now received the ball back.

"Great share." I think. I love a good chest pass. I love any good pass.

And after another dribble or two he dishes the ball to the third boy (Colby), the one who had filled the other lane (on the left), and Colby now drives to the hoop for the uncontested layup.

As he takes his last dribble he shifts the ball from his dominant right hand to his left and launches himself off his right foot toward the hoop, ready to bank the shot off the backboard for an easy two and hopefully notices by the coaches.

"Watch out!" I hear the boy who initially stole the ball yell as that grey streak I had noted somehow catches up to Colby from behind and without fouling him snatches the ball out of Colby's left hand, tucks it into his gut, and carries the ball out of bounds, preventing the easy bucket as his momentum carries him directly into the cold, white, cement wall which he hits with full force and a hollow thud.

"Oh my God! Are you alright?!" I scream within my own head as I start to run toward the now still grey mound on the floor.

But before I can get there (yes, I am pretty slow) the grey mass gets up, chomping on his gum, and slamming the ball into the floor as he jogs back onto the court to take his position on defense.

"What is his number?" I think.

And after many advanced yoga moves to look over, around, under and through the crowd of players, refs and coaches, I see that this grey force of nature is number 43.

"43. He is number 43. But who is #43?" I think as I scan my assessment player list.

"Jimmy. Jimmy Douglason. Number 43." I note.

Back on the court, Jimmy continues to chomp on his gum as he runs stoop shouldered up and down the court harassing ball handlers, blocking passes, diving into the stands, running with the ball with an occasional dribble, and slamming the ball off the backboard like he is trying to shatter it à la Darryl Dawkins (but without the thunder slam).

Jimmy is everywhere. Jimmy never stops. Number 43.
Number 43 is Jimmy. Number 43 is like Superman.

"Jimmy is Superman", I note on my paper.

And then I write … Superman = Heart.

My team needs a Superman.

Chapter 14

Mixing Work and Play

One week I had to travel for business, so my assistant coach was leading the team. And as I was enjoying a quiet dinner after a day full of meetings I received the following text:

"Halftime. Us 19 them 20. David upset."

Once I realized the text came from my assistant coach's wife and that she was in constant communication with her husband, I responded:

"Tell David he will shoot better when he is relaxed. Also tell him to use his aggression under the boards."

I soon inquired about the other team's defense and called an offensive play.

"Basket."

We continued our texting and I learned of a defensive lapse. No problem. It was corrected with a little encouragement from afar.

More information was shared, and I found myself truly engaged in the game and cheering the team on from hundreds of miles away.

Question about an offensive set. No problem. Text.

Team down a bit emotionally. No problem. Text.

And eventually I learned through the wonders of technology that we had won.

But was that the best text I received that night? No.

The best text I received actually came after the game and simply said, "Boys loved hearing from you!"

Technology is a terrific tool … when used to enhance relationship and connection … not to replace it.

Chapter 15

What Fine Young Men

I remember another game a few years back where we were getting beat soundly and our players were feeling down. As I turned to the scoreboard and saw we were trailing 43 to 12 late in the first half, I called our players' attention to it. I called their attention to the fact that the outside world was judging us based on those electric red numbers glaring ... and yet the outside world had no idea the measure of a young man's heart, the real measure of our team's success.

We turned our attention toward each of our own measures of success, each step we were making individually and together to improve as basketball players (and coaches) and as men. We talked about the outside world and the glare of the red and set that aside to focus on the REAL wins, the TRUE measures of success.

Back on the court, the other team continued driving, scoring, pushing, harassing, showboating and taunting. And yet my boys never gave an inch and played with perseverance, tenacity, grit and integrity until the final whistle.

Even though the neon red numbers had grown further and further apart, by the end of the game they no longer glared down on our team. Those numbers were no longer the key metric to be measured against; they were no longer all encompassing.

In fact, the outside world's view changed for that one game and it saw what the glowing red numbers could never show, as exemplified by the two referees approaching me after the game, "Those boys, we have never seen that type of maturity, focus, determination and HEART in all of our years of refereeing than we saw tonight. What an amazing team. What fine young men."

Chapter 16

The Point Guard

Each year we would go through the player assessment and draft process.

And being a recreation basketball league, we would need to redraft an entire new team.

Redrafting

I was blessed that over the years more and more players and their parents would request to become part of our team, our community, our family. This was a testament to each of our players, their parents, their siblings, Coach Sampras and Coach Norgaard (my amazing assistant coaches), and of course my bride and daughters who truly made this a family effort.

In fact, as I would walk into the assessments each year the head of the rec program would clue me in …

"Tom, Mrs. Jackson said her son must be on your team. I let her know I cannot guarantee it and she let me know that if he is not playing for you he won't be playing a sport this Fall and Winter."

This increased year to year until the pressure to select players became quite great as it was no longer only about heart, talent, fit, and bi-directional learning, sharing and contribution. Right or wrong it started to include taking ownership of the fact that if these young men are not selected to be part of this team, some may not have positive experiences in sports, may not learn the greatness of team, may not grow to enjoy physical movement, may not learn to push themselves beyond what they believe themselves capable of, and may not learn and grow in ways that sports can provide that apply to all walks of life.

"Doc, I cannot draft all of these young men. Billy is great but if I ensure Mickey is on the team then Billy's talent and heart is not. But if I select Billy then Mickey will clearly not have the opportunity to learn and grow like I know he can on this team. It is so hard."

"Tom, you cannot save them all. Just do what you think is best. You cannot take on responsibility for those things you cannot control."

Always wonderful wisdom from Doc. I wish I could say it was easy to follow. It was not, and many a tear was shed as I realized that I would disappoint young men regardless of how I selected my team and that each decision would impact a child in one way or another.

And even though I made a special effort to connect directly with each child that I knew wanted to be part of this team but unfortunately I did not or could not select (to talk with them, invite them to Sunday morning basketball, and / or to simply wish them the best) it did not provide relief to me as I knew how special our team was.

And although incredibly challenging to bring together, each player and each team over the years was special. Made so because of the community we built ... together.

Each player was selected for all the reasons above. Each player had many gifts to share with the team. And specific to "on the court gifts" ... we had rebounders, shot blockers, snipers, hustlers, Superman (of course), hop-steppers, up-fakers, screeners, speed-demons, and more ... and many combinations of some or many of these attributes.

Now, as shared previously, in my playing days (a little bit of school ball but mostly church league basketball back in the day), I was not a shooter. In fact, I was always a horrible shooter. But I would out hustle anybody and I could play the point. In my mind, nothing is better than taking charge and doing everything it takes to help others achieve what they never thought possible. And a big part of that is determining when and how (and executing) the perfect pass that sets up a teammate to hit a shot. And I loved making that pass and then watching as a teammate uses their God-given gift (refined with much practice) to drain a J or hit a layup or follow suit with another pass. Now that is true joy on the court. And in my mind, it was a wonderful example of servant leadership.

One specific season, after another challenging player assessment and draft, we again formed a special team. And post draft, as I reviewed the roster with Coaches Sampras and Norgaard, we identified that we were missing something. We were missing … a point guard. The very position I gravitate towards, the floor general, the leader, the player with whom as coach I must have a close working relationship and who must know even above all others what I expect of him and the strategy for each game. Yes, I did not draft … a point guard.

Now, I could say that I simply blew it and "forgot" or "overlooked" this position. But that simply would not be true as I am always on the lookout for this special player … the Bob Cousy of Gorham. Nope. Each of the boys selected for our team was selected for specific reasons and needed to be on our team. I knew this and was grateful they were each available when the time came for me to select. And as noted, they each had wonderful gifts (and areas to learn and improve). They were simply not point guards and I decided that it was too important to have these twelve specific boys together than to select a different player with the point guard skillset.

So here we were, us three coaches together trying to determine who could play the point or how we could play without a point guard. How to modify the offense to adjust to having no true point. How to distribute the ball early and leverage the skills of other players to offset this challenge.

And so began this effort as the preseason started. Early ball distribution with multiple screen sets and working the ball into the post early with a kickback to the sniper if open, along with weak side cuts and strong rebounding … and of course our solid triangle defense which together we developed and implemented over multiple years.

Each practice the team got better and better.

Plays were implemented, each relying on screens and movement … but mostly teamwork. For each player to be successful the team must be successful. And for the team to be successful each player must be successful. Both And. Yes, this was planned. Yes, this was coached. And hopefully the boys have carried this message into their lives beyond the court.

And yet …

As I continued to watch and learn I saw that we were truly missing a floor commander. That one person who could and would take charge with the ball and implement our strategy to position each of the other players to be at their best. We needed a point guard. Our own servant leader on the court. I was not a good enough coach to position this team where they deserved to be without a point guard. We needed a point. But where was I going to find one?

My kingdom for a point guard! (To paraphrase the Bard of Avon).

"Doc, our team is perfect in so many ways. I love these kids. They will go through walls for each other … for the team. We will win more than we lose, and we could make the playoffs.

But we do not have a point guard and be it simply my affinity for the point or a true need … I want a point guard to lead this team to the playoffs."

"What about Tommy?"

What about Tommy? Tommy is my son. Tommy is a phenomenal rebounder. Tommy can shoot and he can pass. What about Tommy? He is a Four or a Five (a power forward or a center) and maybe a Three (a shooting forward). But a guard?

"Doc, Tommy is built to play underneath. I don't want to set him up to fail." That is the last thing I want to do.

"Okay. Then maybe you simply need to coach a team without a point guard."

The Big Kid play the point?

Practice

"Come on dad…we are going to be late."

Clearly it must be the night of our next practice. It is 6:30pm and our practice begins at 7:00.

"Let's go dad!"

It takes less than 5 minutes to get there.

"Dad, where are you? Come on…I don't want to be late! Come on!"

Okay, Tommy. Okay.

We arrive at practice … early. Coach Sampras and Coach Norgaard are already here as are most of the boys and they are ready to scrimmage.

"No, we are not scrimmaging yet! Bring it in! Hold those basketballs!"

I continued …

"Our first game is Saturday morning in Windham. You have all worked very hard and we still have much to do. Tonight, we are working on our '4' in bound play, the box, the stack, and the '10'. We will also be working on our movement offense and the triangle defense. When we are successful with each, we will then scrimmage. Okay, John?"

John, as with all the boys, loves to scrimmage.

"YES, COACH!"

"Let's go! Three lines! Weave! Good chest pass, then bounce pass, and finish by going up strong for the layup. Let's get 20 layups in a row!"

And with that the boys charged into the three lines and began a spirited practice full of much sweat, laughter, hard work, joking, and learning. For all of us.

And 90 minutes later we finished the night with a review of all we learned, a reminder that our first game will be at 9:30am at the Windham High School and a … "Gorham on three!" led by Tommy.

"1 – 2 – 3! … GORHAM!!" The entire team screamed.

And then …

"Thank you, Coach."

"Great practice, Superman."

"Thank you, Coach."

" Excellent rebounding, Mickey T."

"Thank you, Coach."

"Love the hop step, Barry."

Until it was down to Coach Sampras and me.

"Coach, what do you think?"

"Tom, we need a point guard."

"Agreed."

And off we went … with me processing how I could develop a point guard in the next two days.

Game time

It's Saturday morning and the kids are energized. In their North Carolina blue t-shirts, they are excited to play.

"Tommy, I want to talk with you."

"Yeah, Dad."

"I've been watching you a great deal in practice. I have put you at the Three, the Four, the Five and you have played them all very well."

"Thank you, Dad."

"Our team does not have a true point guard."

"I know, Dad."

And then with as much conviction as I could muster … "I want you to play the point today."

As I said this, a number of thoughts went through my head. "Tommy is great down low and in the paint. He has played each position I put him in very well. I don't want to set him up to fail. He is such a good kid. I love my boy. God, please protect my son."

"Okay." Tommy replied.

"Do you know each of the plays?"

"Yes, Dad."

"Do you know the responsibility of the One (the point guard) on each play?"

"Yes, Dad."

"Are you ready to lead this team?"

"Yes."

"Do you want to lead this team?"

"Yes."

"Tommy, go lead this team!"

"Yes, Dad!"

Game On

It is now sixty seconds before tipoff.

"Bring it in!" I yell over the noise of the crowd.

"First game boys. Are you ready?"

"YES COACH!"

"I know you are. Here is the lineup."

And as I read the lineup to the team my mind wanders to the Big Kid and simply wanting my son to get a win.

"Gorham on Three!" Tommy yells.

"1 – 2 – 3 ... GORHAM!!" the team screams.

Tip off

Superman tips the ball back to Tommy. Tommy grabs it, pauses momentarily as he scans the court and then begins to dribble past half court.

"Set Up!" He yells.

"One!" He makes the play call.

The team sets up. Our Four and Five down low. Our Two on the right wing. Our Three on the left. The team is in position.

"Five!" I hear Tommy yell with no prompt from the bench.

He has called the pick and roll play we worked on a thousand times in practice and which calls for the Five (the person playing the center position) to set a screen for the point guard. Tommy would typically set the screen. This time he runs through the screen … perfectly.

The pick and roll works as designed and as Tommy reaches the foul line he looks right to fake the defender and then makes a perfect behind the back pass to the left and hits the Five, Jaryd, who rolled perfectly, for a wide-open layup.

"Bang!" 2 – 0 Gorham.

"Great play, Tommy." I call out to my son.

But he is focused.

The speedy point guard for Windham has the ball now and is on Tommy quick.

This is what I was afraid of.

The speedy point jukes and then crosses over in order to blow by Tommy and hit the lane.

But he doesn't realize Tommy has been practicing his pick pocketing skills and as the point switches hands Tommy comes up from below with his left hand facing up, pokes the ball away from the point and toward half court, and then in one motion runs to the right of the point, grabs the ball, and then sprints with the ball to the other hoop, going up strong so

the point guard who is trying to make a block
cannot make the play, and scores an easy layup.

"Yes, Tommy!" 4 – 0 Gorham.

Now the Windham point guard is ticked off. He was
embarrassed (why I don't know as it was simply a basketball
play) and is now talking a great deal of trash as he comes up
the court.

He crosses midcourt and calls for a screen.

The Windham shooting guard (the Two) runs over toward
Tommy to set a blindside pick as the point guard again
crosses over and this time intends to use the screen.

Unfortunately for the shooting guard, Tommy does not see
the screen (it being an illegal blind side pick) and Tommy
literally blows it up. As Tommy first side steps and then turns
to cut with the Windham point guard he inadvertently drives
his shoulder into the chest of the shooting guard knocking
him off his feet and onto his back 5 feet down the court.

A whistle.

"Foul on number 5, green, (Windham) for an illegal screen.
Gorham ball." The referee calls out.

"Yes! … You okay, Tommy?"

"I'm fine, Dad."

Needless to say, Windham doesn't set any more screens on Tommy. Not that the Windham point guard doesn't call for them. The other players for some reason simply don't set them.

The game continues like this for the remaining thirty-eight minutes. Tommy in complete command. Making passes. Positioning teammates to score. Hustling up and down the court. Weak side rebounding. Whatever it takes. And leading the team to our first win of the season with great contributions from everyone.

"I found a point guard. We found a point guard." I think as the final buzzer goes off.

An apology

After all Tommy had been through over the years … after he was bullied by adults and kids alike, after baseball coaches had overlooked him because of the way God made him, after parents had forbid him from playing with their children because he was "the Big Kid" … and after each of these scenarios Tommy showing more maturity than them all … after all of this … what did I do?

I, too, overlooked the Big Kid.

I overlooked the point guard right in front of me.

I overlooked the heart and soul Tommy brings to all he does … and I am ashamed.

Tonight's tears are being shed because this coach, this father, did what he swore he would never do ... I overlooked my son.

Tommy, I am so sorry.

You are a leader on and off any court and any field. You have greatness inside you and you marry this greatness with a rare humility and caring soul.

I love you ... and again you have taught me.

Thank you for always being there to teach your Dad.

Chapter 17

Above the Fray

Each team I coached was comprised of special young men. Not all easy. Not all basketball superstars. But each one special and each one contributing, learning and teaching one another and of course … me.

We had Mickey T. who simply wanted to be part of this community of young men. A basketball phenom? No. But over time he became the best "rip it" player on the court.

As a reminder, to ensure you secure the ball after a rebound or an interception (or any loose ball for that matter) it is important to not only grab the ball with your hands and arms but to use your full body to "rip" the ball away from the other team.

Mickey T. off the court is very quiet (perhaps another Introvert?), easy going, and mild mannered. On the court he became the player I could most count on to rip the ball from the other team. (As well as to secure key rebounds, make a clutch pass, and to score on occasion.) A player we were blessed to have in our midst. A player we needed on our team.

There are many players like this each year. Each who taught me. Each I will never forget. Many I pray for each day.

Abel is one of these players.

During Tommy's Junior year in High School, as like every other year I coached, we had a player assessment to begin the next Gorham recreational basketball league season. And as always, I stood alone analyzing each player. There were some younger players with amazing skills. There was a Junior who had a big ego and a big game. There was a Senior with a scruffy beard that had some game but more so what caught my attention most was his non-stop hustle during each and every drill. And there were my core players whose parents insisted remain on this team, if at all possible, and who beyond question are all key parts of our community.

As I strolled around the gym looking for kids with heart the head of the rec department approached me.

"Tom, please add the name Abel to your list of potential players. He is a senior. He could not be here for the assessment. I hear he is a pretty good player."

"Okay." I responded as I jotted A-B-E-L down on the back of my paper.

During the actual drafting phase Coach Sampras and I were able to re-acquire the bulk of our core team as well as pick up the Senior with the scruffy beard, Julian. Intentionally I opted to not draft the Junior with the big game and big ego. His talent was unquestionable. And it was a hard choice to allow another team to draft him. But it was also the right decision.

By the end of the draft there were only a couple of player names left on the list, including Abel.

"Tom, would you be willing to take Abel on your team. He has had a rough time of it and I believe your team would be a good fit for him."

"Sure", I responded to the rec leader. "I am happy to add Abel to the team. We only have one other Senior (Julian) so the additional [hopefully] leadership will be a bonus."

"Great. And with that you have your teams. Please contact all your players and let them know. As always they will be anxious to hear from you."

And then after everyone else had filed out of the draft room the rec leader approached me once again.

"Tom, it is important that Abel is on your team. He really has had a tough time of it. In fact, he often sleeps at his father's business rather than at home in his own bed. I am sorry to ask you. But it is important for him."

Little did I know how important Abel joining our team would be for us … for me.

A few days later …

"Come on dad…we are going to be late."

Clearly it must be the night of our first practice.

It is 6:30pm and our practice begins at 7:00.

"Let's go dad!"

It takes less than 5 minutes to get there.

"Dad, where are you? Come on…I don't want to be late! Come on!"

Okay, Tommy. Okay.

We arrive at practice. Coach Sampras is already there as is most of the boys.

And so is Mike the custodian who over the years has become a good friend of the team.

"Tom, coffee is all made for you. Stay as late as you want. Let me know anything you need."

"Thanks, Mike. Great to see you again. We will be here every Tuesday and Friday night for practice just like last year."

"I'll be here. And your coffee will always be ready for you. Just the way you like it."

God brings people into your life for specific reasons. Over the years Mike has become a true friend and confidant for me. He has a good heart and a kind soul. He too became part of our team. Our community. Our family.

"Hey, Coach. Ready to get back at it?"

"Absolutely, Coach."

"Excellent, Pete. Let's do something great!"

And then ...

"Bring it in! Hold those basketballs!"

Nothing quite like the mandarin of bouncing basketballs stopping all at once as the squeal of sneakers heightens and young men race to embrace a new season. A new beginning.

"I'm Coach Dahlborg. This is Coach Sampras. I am thrilled to have you all on this team. Many of you are returning. Some are new. I selected each of you for specific reasons. You are each meant to be on this team."

Then a deep breath and ...

"A few lessons for you. Lesson one: You play the game my way or you don't play. Lesson two: When Coach Sampras or I talk to you, you look us directly in the eyes. Lesson three: This is a team game. You will improve your game. And as you do our team will improve."

"Understood?"

"Yes, Coach!"

"Great, now starting with Tommy", it's hard to be the coach's son, "I want you to introduce yourselves."

And one by one each did. Name. Sometimes they included their position. And usually added a big smile and/or laugh.

"Alright. Three lines! Let's go! Weave!"

Both Julian and Abel pick up the weave quickly. And Julian continued to show here in practice what I saw during the assessment. "Yes!"

And then I focused on Abel. About five foot six. Hair cut very short. Athletic build.

"Let's see what you got, Abel. You got game?"

No verbal response. Just a smirk. And then … a double crossover, 360-degree spin, and then with the grace of my oldest daughter Samantha on the stage for her dance recital finale, a switch from his strong right hand to his left for a Walt Frazier-esque layup.

"Yup, he's got game. It's obvious. He's got game. Now does he have heart? And can he lead?" I ponder.

"Abel, bring it in."

"Yeah, Coach." He responds with that ever-present smirk.

"Nice move. Play the point?"

"Yes, Coach." More smirks.

Tommy has become a very good point guard. He is also a great Three. Finding another point guard and moving Tommy back to the three would be amazing.

"We'll see. Go prove to me that the point is yours."

"Yes, Coach." Another smirk.

This is going to be fun.

Ninety minutes later …

"Bring it in! Very nice first practice. Tommy?"

"Gorham on three!"

"1 – 2 – 3 … GORHAM!!" The team yells and then packs to head out for the evening.

"Well, Coach, we've got another point guard."

"We sure do, Tom. We sure do."

"Tommy, you ready to go back to the Three and show off your scoring touch?"

"Oh, yes, Dad. Oh yeah."

"We will need you at the point too, so be sure you know the One and the Three."

"You got it."

It was an amazing season. With many challenges on and off the court.

"Abel, you missed a practice. You will not be playing the next game."

"Yes. Coach." A smaller smirk.

"Abel. Why did you miss the game on Saturday?"

"I was sick, Coach."

"You need to call me and let me know prior to the game. These boys were counting on you. The team is counting on you. No call next time (if there is a next time) and you will not play in the following game either. Understood?"

"Yes, Coach." No smirk.

"We need you, Abel. But you must be here for this team heart and soul or you will not remain on this team. Understood?"

"Yes, Coach."

Later that night after practice.

"Doc, Abel is a special kid. He has that "IT" factor that they say JFK had. He is a true leader in the sense that people will follow him. Good or bad path they will follow his lead."

"Tom, I understand he is having a real tough time at home."

"I know. I don't want to lose him. I don't mean from the team. I don't want to lose him to the bad path. He is a good kid. It is so hard to be tough on him knowing how rough he has it."

"I think he needs that discipline … that adult figure that cares enough about him to discipline him."

"Thank you, Doc. I needed to hear that. This is very hard."

Several weeks later it is our second playoff game and we are competing with a strong and chippy team from Windham on their home court. We are up by seven late in the second half and the team is playing well. And Abel is leading them.

Tommy has dropped ten. Mickey T. has another six. Abel has seventeen while also passing the rock and getting everyone involved. There are contributions from all over.

"A steal! Abel has stolen the ball with three minutes to go!"

I am doing play by play in my own head.

"That's it, Abel. Go!" I call out.

With his great speed Abel is over half court in no time with all but one defender trailing far behind. As he reaches the elbow he crosses over from left to right juking the last line of defense and begins to go up with his patented Frazier when the defender who was clearly beaten makes a hard foul and knocks Abel to the floor and into the wall behind the hoop.

A whistle.

"Foul. Number 8, Green. Two shots!" The ref calls out.

But while the ref is explaining the call and why two shots and not two shots and the ball for a flagrant, I see Abel in the face of the defender who committed the hard foul and then pointing up at the score board.

"Time out! Time out!" I yell to the ref over the noise of the crowd. "Bring it in, boys. Everyone else up off the bench. Bring it in!"

"Abel, are you okay?"

"Yes, Coach." No smirk.

"Good. Now listen to me and listen good. We are up. It is late in the game. Do not lose your composure."

"He was mouthing off to me. So, I simply pointed up to the scoreboard and reminded him of who was winning."

God, I wanted to laugh. Yup … thirty years ago (who am I kidding) last week I would have done the same thing.

"I understand. Now listen to me. Everyone. Listen Up! We need all of you if we are going to win this game. We do not lose control. We play smart. We play together. We stay above the fray. Do you understand?"

"YES, COACH!"

And then as half of the team heads back onto the court and the other half back to the bench I pull Abel aside.

"Abel, look at me, do you understand?"

"Yes, Coach." No smirk.

"We need you. Go hit your free throws and lead us to victory."

A smile.

Abel hit his two free throws and made two more steals. He dished the rock. He scored another four points and we increased our lead and we won this playoff game.

"Great game, Team!"

And then after folks began to depart.

"Abel, ABOVE THE FRAY. Always. Got it?"

"Yes, Sir."

"I am proud of you."

Chapter 18

Most Assuredly a Win

"Bobby dropped 21? Fantastic!"

Yes. I meant it. Bobby scoring 21 was fantastic. If only I was there to see it.

Tommy and I had been gifted tickets to go and see the Boston Celtics, (yes, the team of Russell, Heinsohn, Cousy, Bird, Lewis), at the TD Garden in Boston, and the game happened to fall on a day of one of our Gorham High School Recreation basketball games.

"Doc, I cannot go to Boston to see the Celtics. I can't let the team down."

"Tom, you have been coaching for over seven years. You have rushed home from Boston after intensely stressful workdays to coach when you really should have been taking care of yourself better. This Celtics game is for you and Tommy. A gift. You need this. This will be good for you two. Pete can coach the team."

There was no doubt in my mind that Pete can coach the team. Pete Sampras and I have coached for years together. He is a caring and smart man. He would be fine.

And yet ... and yet it is my responsibility and it is my job. (My non-paying and most rewarding job I have ever had.)

"Honey ..."

"Don't you honey me. You just call Pete, let him know he is coaching on Saturday, and you and Tommy go to the Celtics game together and have a relaxing and good time. Do you understand?"

Doc is so Brockton-tough when she chooses to be. (Don't tell her I said that.)

"Pete, Saturday Tommy and I will not be at the basketball game. We were gifted tickets to the Celtics. Would you mind taking over head coaching duties that day? I will ensure Coach Norgaard will be available to assist."

"Of course, no problem, Tom."

He is such a good man. A good father. A good coach. A good leader. A good friend.

"We are playing the Bonny Eagle team with the big front court. We will need to be solid on the boards."

"Tom, don't worry. We will be fine."

And then a few days later after practice …

"Pete, we are well-positioned for the playoffs. But a win Saturday will help our seeding. Here is the lineup tool I use. It might assist you with your substitution strategy."

"Thanks, Tom."

"All I will say is … Coach the team as YOU would coach them. The kids respect you and, as you know, will play hard for you."

The day of the game

So now it is Saturday and Tommy and I are driving down 95 South on our way to Boston.

"Tommy, text Laura." Pete's wife. "She will be watching the game for sure. Let's see how the team is doing."

"Okay, Dad."

I keep thinking to myself that I should be there. It is my responsibility.

"Dad, Laura says we are down 5 with 6 minutes left in the first half."

"Down five without Tommy (one of our best scorers) there. That is great," I think to myself.

"Excellent."

"She says David is having a huge game. Rebounding and scoring big."

"Fantastic."

I knew these boys wouldn't shrink without their coach and without Tommy. These boys have heart. Always did.

"Barry did a hop step and hit a shot after a steal by Bobby!"

"This is great," I think as Laura continues to give Tommy the play by play as we are entering New Hampshire.

"Best hop-stepper ever!" I say.

"Dad, they tied it up. They tied it up with thirty seconds left in the first half. Bobby hit a three from the corner to tie it up!"

Both Tommy and I were getting excited. Truly technology is a good thing (when used right). And with Laura texting us updates, Tommy and I both feel like we are there.

"Dad, Mrs. Sampras said we are tied at half time. She says David is being an animal underneath the boards, Dean already has 4 blocked shots, Mickey T. has ripped the ball away from the other team a number of times, and Bobby has already scored ten points."

I must admit, for a moment I did think, "they don't need me". I wish I didn't. I wish I did not go to the selfish place in my mind. I wish I simply was able to enjoy what I was hearing. And yet ... I did go to that place.

"Are you kidding me?" I said to myself as I fought with my own ego. "Get over yourself. This is not about you. Look at Tommy. He is relishing the success of his peers. Be like Tommy."

And then ...

"God. Please help me," I prayed as I took a deep breath and allowed His spirit to pass over me like a wave, washing away all those unproductive thoughts.

"Dad. Do you think the team can win?"

Now how do I answer that seemingly innocuous question? I don't want Tommy to think for one second, he is not important to the team.

"Coach Sampras and the boys are really playing their hearts out. The team they are facing is tough and to be tied at halftime without your leadership and heart is impressive. Do I think we can win? Yes. But it is going to be very hard."

"I think we are going to win." Tommy responds.

He is such a good kid. And it is still amazing to me how much my son, "the Big Kid" who was so bullied, so hurt, so harmed, by so many, has grown and matured and cares so very much about others. He truly loves this team. He truly loves his teammates … his friends. He would do anything for them.

"Dad, Mrs. Sampras says that both Julian and Abel are not playing. Both are out sick."

Basketball season is a tough time of year for kids and colds.

"Just think about that, Tommy. Coach Sampras and the team are tied at halftime against one of the better teams even though we are missing three very good players, Julian, Abel, and you. Think about that."

"That's awesome, Dad."

"That is why we draft for heart. Heart keeps you in games when your mind says it is impossible. Coach Sampras is doing an amazing job leading the team, and the boys are doing their jobs and not backing down. Heart."

And we both sat in silence thinking about that as we continued our trek south … each of us missing our team.

"Dad, Mrs. Sampras said David just fouled out. She said he played a huge game and even hit a three pointer. But is now out of the game."

"Come on, Pete. Come on." I think as I try to send encouragement to Coach Sampras through the ethers of time and space.

"David is a beast, but sometimes he gets stuck in the fray of the game. This time, however, it sounds like he played a phenomenal game. How much time is left?"

"Six minutes, Dad."

"Score?"

"We are down four."

"Amazing, Pete." I think. "Just amazing."

"Tommy, you are down four key players. You are playing against a solid team with a big front court. What would you do?"

"I'd stack the triangle defense we use with Mickey T., Dean, and John. I would put Mark at the point and set Bobby up for the three on offense. No one gets inside. And with the limited players I would not press. Need to save legs for the final few minutes."

"God he is good. Love this kid," I think to myself.

"Tommy, are you okay not being there?"

"I am not going to lie, Dad. I wish I was there."

"Me too." I respond softly. "I wish we were both there." And then after a brief pause, "And … I am glad we are here together witnessing the greatness of our team in a whole new way, appreciating the team in a whole new way … AND … we are going to have a great time together at the Celtics game."

"Exactly, Dad."

More silence as we continue our journey.

"Dad! Bobby just hit another three-pointer. He now has 21 points!"

"Bobby dropped 21? Fantastic! What is the score now?"

"We are down three with 30 seconds to go."

"This is so exciting. Now I would press, go for the steal and if no steal foul quickly. With no shot clock and time running out we need the ball back. And the Bonny Eagle team has not been great from the foul line. Got to risk it."

"Mrs. Sampras says Bonny Eagle just scored again. She says we look tired. Down five now with 16 seconds left."

"I bet the kids are exhausted," I respond to Tommy thinking about the hill they are climbing this day.

And then I think to myself, "Call timeout, Pete. Call timeout. Set a play for Bobby for the three, if not there dump it inside quickly to Dean for the two and possibly a foul."

"Dad, we lost. Mrs. Sampras said we got the ball past half court, they trapped us, but Mark got it inside to Dean who hit a two as time expired. We lost by three. Dad, we lost."

We lost? I don't think so. If any game was a win. That was it. This game was most assuredly a win.

Chapter 19

Here Comes His Dad

"Darian, come here. We have three minutes left in the game. We are down five points. I want you to run the '3'. Do you know the '3'?"

"No, Coach."

My mind started racing. "I want to get Darian back into the game, but he doesn't know the play. I only have a few seconds to decide what to do. I don't want to mishandle this situation. If I put him in and we run the play that I believe will best position the team to win he won't know what to do. I don't have time to instruct him on the play. He has missed a number of practices. I want all my players to have equal playing time. The '10' could work but not as well as the '3'.

Yes, so many thoughts firing all at once.

"Darian, take a seat. I will talk to you after the game. Mickey T! You are in. Tell Tommy to run the '3'"

"Okay, Coach."

As Mickey runs across the court I am still thinking about Darian. "Did I embarrass him? Did I hurt his feelings? What else could I do? If I played him and either ran the '3', the play he doesn't know, or the '10', the play that is less effective, wouldn't each harm the team?"

And as I am still processing my conversation with Darian … play on the court continues.

David inbounds the ball to Tommy. Tommy runs through the screen set by Mickey T. Mickey then rolls toward the hoop as designed but the defense makes a nice switch so that he is now covered. The defense swarms as Tommy drives the lane and as they double-team him he makes a "no-look" behind the back pass to Ricky who has driven the baseline.

Ricky gathers the rock with two hands and then goes up strong with his right.

"Score!" Coach Sampras yells.

"And a foul!" Coach Norgaard adds.

We are now down three points with just over two minutes to go and Ricky is at the line.

"Tommy! When Ricky hits his free throw, I want you to press using the '5'. Got it? The '5'. Full court press. Get the steal. Get that ball back. Got it?" I call out to Tommy who is playing the point and leading the team brilliantly.

"Got it, Coach." Tommy responds.

Ricky hits his free throw. We are now down two.

And Tommy yells so that even his grandparents hundreds of miles away on Cape Cod can hear, "FIVE! FIVE! FIVE!"

The team sets up the press.

"Yes!" I think.

And seeing it the coach of the other team calls … "Time out!"

"Bring it in!" I call out. And then, "Everyone up off the bench too."

And as the fighting five on the court run over to the huddle I am still thinking about Darian.

"Okay, same five are still in," I say to the team.

The snake has worked well, and everyone has had equal playing time, except for Darian now.

"Okay. Team, we got them thinking. This time we are not going to press."

I then continue, "We have two minutes left. We are down two." And then turning to Coach Sampras, "What is our foul situation?"

"We are in the penalty. But no one is at risk of fouling out. The closest are Tommy, Dean and David. Each with three."

"Thanks, Coach." I respond.

And then focusing back on the team, "I want Tommy and Jimmy to harass the ball handlers about three-quarters of the way up the court. Rest of the team back on D shutting down the lane. I am not too concerned about a foul as they have not been great from the line. That said, Tommy and Jimmy force the ball handler to the sidelines."

And then turning to Dean and looking him directly in the eyes, "Dean, you watch and play free safety. If the ball handler is forced to the right sideline I want you ready to intercept the long pass to that same side. And same thing on the left sideline. Understood?"

"Got it, Coach."

"David, no middle. Understood?"

"Yes, Coach."

"We got this. Tommy …"

"Gorham on Three!"

I love when he does this.

"One! Two! Three! ... GORHAM!!" The entire team yells.

Back on the court the other team in-bounds the ball under their own basket.

With our press disengaged they appear surprised.

"Let's go, Tommy!" I hear Doc yell from the stands.

Tommy and Jimmy double the point guard just before half court and force him to the right sideline with their great footwork and teamwork.

And just after he crosses half court they trap him.

"Yes!" I hear from somewhere behind me.

As they do, I see Dean begin creeping over toward the right sideline ready for the intercept if in fact the pass is thrown that way.

"There it is!" I think as the point guard, under duress due to the defensive pressure, jumps into the air and tries to launch a pass down the sideline a la Mark Sanchez.

(Sorry Jets fans.)

"Go Dean!" I hear Coach Sampras call out as Dean plays the pass perfectly and times his leap to make the interception.

"Perfect!" I think as I watch Dean not only intercept the ball but also pass the ball to Mickey T. prior to landing out of bounds and in the stands himself.

"Great play, Dean!" Coach Norgaard yells.

As the ball gets to Mickey a defender tries to snatch it away from him. But for years Mickey has been our "rip it" guy and here again he rips the ball away from the defense and makes a solid pass to Tommy.

We now have just over one-minute left in the game and are still down two points.

"Set up! 3! 3!" Tommy takes charge on the court and calls the three again.

Mickey comes up and sets a hard pick for Tommy who then frees himself by running through the pick just as he has been coached.

Mickey rolls to the hoop perfectly keeping himself facing the ball the entire time.

As the defense collapses onto Tommy he dishes the ball to Mickey who is now wide open in the paint.

Mickey doesn't catch the ball cleanly and is a bit off balance as he tries to put the shot up quickly.

The ball hits backboard and then clangs off the rim.

"Rebound!" I think, as Dean, who has gotten back into the play having extricated himself from the sidelines after the steal, comes out of nowhere to sky over the defensive players under the boards, grab the ball and put it back up.

"Score! We tied the game!" Coach Sampras yells as the ball goes through the net.

"Great play, Team!" I call out.

And then I add, "Time out!"

In the huddle, "Team, they have twenty seconds to try to win this game in regulation. That is not going to happen. This is our game. And we are going to win it right now."

As I say this I am still thinking about Darian, "Should I put him in?"

But I choose not to. I decide to keep the continuity on the court.

I continue, "They are going to try to get the ball to number 4, their best ball handler and quickest player."

God how I appreciate Coach Sampras' scouting reports.

"We are not going to let them. We are pressing. Jimmy and Dean, you are doubling number 4. Tommy you have their other guard, number 8."

Turning to Mickey T., "Mickey T, you are on ball. I want to see you harass, harass, harass. Arms up and waving frantically. Do not give him a clear passing angle of any kind. You can do it. Understand?"

"Yes, Coach."

"Ricky, you have the midcourt. You are now our strong safety. Our Ronnie Lott [but without the hitting]. If they try to throw to midcourt you will pick it off. And David, you are playing prevent defense. Anything past Ricky is yours. Both of you watch their quarterback's eyes. He is throwing it to where he is looking."

As I said previously, I played football back in the day. Hopefully my mixing of sports lingo does not confuse.

"Understand, boys?"

"Yes, Coach."

"Tommy ..."

"Gorham on Three!"

Yes, I do so love when he does this.

Our team sets up.

Mickey T. is frantically jumping and waving his arms.

The double team is frustrating number 4.

Tommy is fronting number 8 so that the only pass that would work is a lob … and Dean is all ready for that.

"Timeout!" The other coach yells out as he throws his scorebook on the floor.

"Yes!" I say out loud. And then, "Bring it in!"

"Okay, team. That was perfect. Absolutely perfect. So here is what we are going to do now…"

I pause as I look into the eyes of each of these warriors. The players on the bench right now who got us to this point and these five on the court. Each of them.

And then I see Darian and I look into his eyes.

And my heart begins to break a little.

"But I can't let the team down," I think. "Focus!" I say to myself.

Turning to the team, "We are going to ... breathe. When you go back on the court you will do the exact same thing you just did. We are not changing. They are changing for us. We are not changing for them. This is our game and we are winning it right here. So, as they strategize and come up with a new way to try to get the ball in ... just breathe and enjoy this moment. Being in this huddle as a team with this excitement ... this is heaven. Enjoy this moment."

And for that next minute we did. We simply stood together in a circle and breathed in the moment. Cherishing it.

"Let's go Gorham." The ref called out to me as the other team begins to make its way back on the court ...

"Tommy ..."

"Gorham on Three!"

And then we set up just as before.

I notice they have switched out quarterbacks, but Mickey T. has him covered.

"No worries," I think to myself.

"Balls in," I think as the referee hands the ball to the other team.

They have five seconds to get the ball in play and then another eight seconds to get it past half court.

I begin to count in my head, "One, two, three ..."

Balls not in. No passing lanes are available.

Number 4 then tries to split the double team and run a fly a la Randy Moss.

With one second left out of his five, their new QB decides to throw the ball deep toward number 4.

"Yes! Just what we wanted," I think.

Here comes both Ricky and Dean. Dean fronts number 4 and Ricky seeing the pass is coming in short (due to the pressure applied by Mickey T) jumps in front of the pass and intercepts the ball.

"Yes!" I yell ... along with everyone else on our sidelines.

I think quickly and opt to not call a timeout.

The pressure we applied has well-positioned three of our players in the front court.

Ricky collects himself. And as he does David sets a pick on number 4 to prevent a steal.

Jimmy then sets a screen for Tommy, so he can go to the ball.

"That's our Superman. Way to play selflessly, Jimmy!" I think.

Seeing Tommy break free, Ricky fires a chest pass to Tommy who without looking (at least it looked that way to me) fires a baseball throw to Dean who has V cut his way away from the defense and is now driving toward the hoop.

The clock is ticking down. Five, Four, Three, …

The pass hits Dean in the hands and in stride. And all in one motion he lays the ball softly off the glass and into the hoop as time expires.

"We Win! We Win!" I hear our team chant as our players rush off the bench to celebrate with the five on the court.

"We Win! We Win!" I hear our fans in the stands saying over and over.

"Yes!" I say in my head as I look up at the scoreboard and see that it is official. "Game over. We win."

And yet … and yet, I don't feel much like celebrating. "Where is Darian?" I wonder.

"Pete, have you seen Darian?"

"No. Not since the game ended. But here comes his Dad."

Chapter 20

The Fleeting Moments

Sometimes the memory of a win lasts.

Years prior …

"We have them on the run. Now it is time to finish the job. Go back out there and take this game. No one gets inside! This is our game. Now take it!"

We were in the midst of a tough losing streak and this morning we were going against the other Gorham basketball team on a brand new hard court in a brand new elementary school built across town.

The other Gorham team was very talented and very vocal. We at this point had not found our footing.

The game began with the other team scoring a quick four buckets and thus we were down eight when Tommy called over to me.

"Dad, I think this is a girl's ball."

"What?"

These games were very well attended, and the acoustics were not very good in the gym.

"Dad! I think the basketball is too small. I think it is a girl's ball!"

It finally registered to me what Tommy was saying.

"Ref. Ref!" I called over to the referee.

I did not want to waste a timeout but would if necessary.

"Ref!"

"Coach?"

"I believe the game ball is too small. Please check it."

"Too small?"

The ref, who I knew very well from our many years in this league together, proceeded to blow his whistle and ask for the ball from Tommy, who was about to shoot two free throws after being fouled.

He then handed it to me, "Coach? What do you think?"

The ball certainly felt small, but it wasn't until I rolled it in my hands and spied the inflation size that I was able to confirm that yes, Tommy was right. This was the wrong size ball for our league.

"Too small, Ref. Wrong ball."

"What's going on?!?!" The coach of the other Gorham team yelled as I asked Coach Sampras to retrieve an appropriately sized game ball from our bag of basketballs.

"Wrong ball, Coach." Came the response from the ref.

"What do you mean 'wrong ball'? My team is doing just fine with it."

"Ball is too small, Coach. We are replacing it," I said.

I thought for a split second to request a restart to the game due to the fact that a wrong ball was being used and my teams' first few shots were way off the mark, even from Tommy who has become quite the sniper.

But ended up thinking the better of it. In fact, I decided to use this as a motivator. And thus, decided to call a timeout anyway at this point.

"Time out! Bring it in! And everyone up off the bench."

And then after all the boys and Coach Sampras were huddled, "We are only a minute and a half into the game and we are down eight. Our shots have been way off."

I paused as I looked into the eyes of each of our players.

And then continued, "To this point we have been using the wrong ball."

And then looking at Tommy, "Nice catch picking up on it, Tommy."

"Clearly they prefer the wrong ball. We do not."

I made sure I again looked into the eyes of each of my players.

"The rest of the game we are using the proper ball. The rest of the game our shots will be dropping. The rest of the game is ours."

And then again looking at Tommy, "Tommy …"

"Gorham on 3, one, two, three …", Tommy screamed over the sound of the crowd.

"GORHAM!!!!" The team yelled.

For the next thirty-seven minutes or so the teams went back and forth until …

"We have them on the run. Now it is time to finish the job. Go back out there and take this game. No one gets inside! This is our game. Now take it!"

And we did. With Joey finishing the game off with a steal and breakaway layup to put us up by five and seal the victory as the game clock struck zero.

"We win! We win!" I heard chanted from the bench.

"Gorham wins! Gorham wins!" I heard chanted from the crowd.

And as I looked across the way I saw my bride looking at me and smiling as I walked slowly to the other end of the bench to take a seat and a breather as I exhaustedly said to myself, "The losing streak is over. It is finally over. Thank, God. Thank you, God."

Again, sometimes the memory of a win remains.

Back to this night and Darian ...

Unfortunately, not on this particular evening.

Yes, Ricky had made a terrific pass to Tommy who subsequently found Dean who ended up winning the game in regulation with a terrific v-cut and layup.

And yet, at this time I was seeking Darian as his father approached me.

"Coach, I would like to talk with you."

"Sure. Let's talk over here."

I led Darian's father to the far side of our bench and beside the stands where we could have a little bit of privacy.

"Coach, you screwed up and now my son is hurting."

"I am so sorry to hear that, Mr. Lovell."

Mr. Lovell proceeded to tell me what a lousy coach I was. How I harmed his son's psyche. How I owe him and his son an apology. And much more.

Still processing what had occurred I stood quietly and let Mr. Lovell speak his peace and then simply replied, "I will talk to Darian. Thank you for letting me know."

Mr. Lovell then walked away, clearly not satisfied, as I stood reliving the Brian Boxswain E-mail from so long ago.

"Tom, you screwed up and you hurt a kid. You screwed up," was all I could think as I slowly walked back to the bench to deliver a final message to the team and then find my bride and girls.

Compartmentalizing the Lovell conversation while now speaking to the team was not easy and the echoes of the past were now pounding loudly in my head.

"Solid win team. And I mean that … team. Every one of you contributed. Every one of you. I am so very proud of the effort, focus, intensity, and support of one another. Win or lose I am proud of what you did on the court this evening."

I was losing my focus so decided to turn to the pragmatic.

"Our next practice is an optional one on Friday evening. 7pm at the Narragansett School. The next regular practice is Monday evening, also at 7pm at the Narragansett School. Any questions?"

"No Coach." Came the reply from all.

"Tommy…"

"Gorham on 3, one, two, three …", Tommy screamed.

"GORHAM!!!!" The team yelled.

"Good game, Coach."

"Thank you, Pete. You too."

"You okay?"

"Yes, Pete. I am fine."

I lied.

Later that evening …

"Tom, are you okay?" Doc asked as we sat together in front of the fireplace.

"I screwed up and I hurt, Darian. Mr. Lovell was very clear. I screwed up."

"No Tom. No. You did your best. You needed to focus on the entire team. And that is what you did. And you did so within a split second."

"But Doc. It wasn't good enough. I hurt a kid. It is my job to focus on the individuals AND the team. Both And. I screwed up."

And as I said this, I repeated over and over in my mind, "I hurt a kid. I hurt a kid. The one thing above all others I swore I would not do. I hurt a kid."

"Oh God," I prayed. "I hurt a kid. Help me make amends. Help me…"

A few days later …

Darian was not at the optional practice on Friday evening.

"Okay, boys. Bring it in. Great game Tuesday night. So tonight … we … are … going … to … … SCRIMMAGE!!"

The team erupts into a cadence of 'scrimmage, scrimmage, scrimmage' and for the next ninety minutes or so we did just that. We played the game as a team with great joy and passion … while also remaining cognizant of improvement opportunities.

And for these ninety minutes the thought of Darian almost left my mind.

Fast forward five years …

"Tom, it is time to go. Kenny Kaplan's graduation party is starting, and we are going to walk over."

"Okay, Doc."

Being an extreme introvert, it is very challenging to get motivated to attend an event where there is a crowd of people. Even when I care for these people.

When we arrived …

"Welcome. Tommy is already here, and Kenny will be so happy that you both came to his party," said Kenny's dad Donald, who is a great person … and brilliant.

Doc and I spoke to Donald for a bit, then to Kenny's mom Charlotte, who like Donald was also very busy with the party, and then finally to Kenny before we grabbed a beverage and headed over to the bonfire.

"What a great party. And there is Tommy with his friends playing whiffle ball," Doc said as she pointed across the way where Tommy was about to unleash his curveball.

"I am just glad you are with me my love."

"Now Tom," came Doc's reply as we both watched some of the neighborhood men carrying logs to expand the fire.

As Doc and I were making some small talk with some of the other party goers, suddenly her fingernails dug into my arm and she leaned in close, "Tom, the Lovell's are here. Mr. Lovell is walking this way."

Even five years later I still had not gotten over the evening that I hurt one of my players.

Yes, I did speak to Darian at the next regular practice after that fateful game … but I always knew that I had screwed up.

"Coach!" I heard Mr. Lovell say as he was approaching from behind us.

I slowly turned expecting to again hear what a lousy coach I was when I saw … a smile?

"Coach! So great to see you," Mr. Lovell said as he outstretched his arm toward me.

And taking his hand in mine I hesitantly responded, "Very nice to see you, too."

Yes, I lied again. For five years I have processed and reprocessed that evening.

"I wanted to tell you …"

"Here it comes," I thought.

"How much Darian enjoyed playing for you …"

"What?!?!" I thought.

"… how much you impacted his life."

"Excuse me?!?! I hurt Darian. I screwed up. I hurt him," my mind reeled.

"And how much Brenda and I appreciate all you did for him."

I truly had no idea what was happening. Nor clearly what happened five years ago.

Mr. Lovell continued, "Darian never played basketball again after that year because he said if you were not his coach then he simply would not play."

"Well, that is not good," I thought.

"And he focused on other interests and is now going off to college."

"How wonderful. Does he have a major selected?"

I was unsure how to respond so thought inquiry would be helpful or at least buy me some time.

"Darian is very interested in politics and law and has decided to attend Brown University in their pre-law program."

We spoke for perhaps another ten minutes or so but honestly, I don't recall much of what more was said as my mind kept going back five years.

And after Mr. Lovell departed I turned to Doc, "What just happened?"

"You see. You see. You stress yourself out all the time and you have no idea the impact you have on these young men."

I still was not ready to hear it. I know what happened five years ago.

"Mr. Lovell was just being nice."

"Tom, sometimes you just have to accept."

Again, I wasn't ready.

About an hour later Doc and I had thanked Charlotte and Donald for the invitation and were now making our way around their house to the street when I heard once again, "Coach!"

But this time it was not Mr. Lovell … it was Darian.

"Darian, I did not see you here. How are you?"

"I am great, Coach."

Not knowing where this was going I braced myself.

"Coach, I wanted to thank you. I loved playing for you …"

I honestly did not hear much more of what Darian shared at this time. And am so thankful that Doc was with me to ensure conversation flowed.

All I know was that five years of regrets for my mistake began to melt off of my heart as this young man said, "You held me accountable. You taught me discipline. I loved playing for you. Thank you, Coach."

"Thank you, God."

Chapter 21

The Discussion

"Tom, the marijuana today is not the same as the marijuana of ten or twenty years ago. It is far more lethal, does far more damage to children, and much of it is laced with other agents to do even more harm."

Working in Boston for the National Institute for Children's Health Quality (NICHQ) I was engaged in a wide variety of healthcare quality improvement initiatives to improve the health of children throughout the country.

And recently, we at NICHQ were approached by a very engaging business leader who lost his son to suicide after his son's long battle with addiction.

"Tom, today's marijuana is a gateway drug to even more harmful drugs. Whatever you can do, you must do to stop a child from using."

As a coach of a high school recreation basketball team I had learned the X's and O's of the game. I had leveraged my leadership and organizational skills. I had failed a lot and I also had some successes by working with Coach Sampras and Coach Norgaard, many parents, the league director, our amazing sponsors, our wonderful players and many others.

But this was different.

I had recently learned that one of my players had begun to smoke marijuana quite frequently and was now trying to entice other players on our team to do so too. And it was breaking my heart.

All my players are special to me and this boy especially so.

But what was I to do? Do I tell his mother, who is also very dear to me? Do I confront him? Is a child smoking marijuana not a big deal anymore in this day and age? Is it none of my business? Is it my responsibility?

With this now threatening to impact my entire team the last two questions were easier to answer.

That said, I struggled to be sure.

Back at NICHQ we were partnering with the business leader and in the process of engaging experts from around the country to develop a quality improvement model to address adolescent drug addiction.

And I was blessed to have developed a relationship with Christy, one of our addiction experts. She was the one sharing her thoughts with me.

"But Christy, this boy is not my child. I am just his coach."

"Tom, the risk is too high, the danger is too great. You must act."

But what if I make things worse?

Upon arriving back in Maine, I discussed this child and what I should do a great deal with my bride.

"The addiction experts we engaged are very clear. I must act. I am going to talk with Clay tonight at practice."

"What are you going to say, Tom?"

"I don't know yet. I am going to pray about it, think about what Christy and the other experts suggested, and when I am ready, sit Clay down."

"I will be praying for you."

"Thank you, my love."

As I drove to practice that evening Tommy was talking about our last game. A game in which we won for many reasons including the fact that he continued his boxing out and rebounding ways, Dean continued to 'set records' blocking shots, Abel was the floor general, and everyone as always contributed.

"Dad, I am going to drop 15 next game. Guaranteed."

I truly loved Tommy's confidence and swagger as he has continued to learn and improve his game, but tonight my mind was elsewhere.

Upon arriving at the Narragansett school ...

"Tom, your coffee is all set in the teacher's dining room. I have a cup on the countertop near the sink for you. And the cream is in the refrigerator as usual."

"Thank you, Mike. And how are you this evening?"

Mike was the custodian at the Narragansett school where we practiced. And over the years we have become quite close.

"A few more hours here, then another five at my next job, and then after that home in front of the TV. Life can't get better than that."

"Wow," I thought, "home by 3am. And yet always so happy."

"Hope you will have a big steak waiting for you when you get home."

"You know it! Now remember, you and your team can stay right up until 10pm if you would like. They are all good kids."

"Yes. Yes, they are," I thought.

"Thank you, Mike. I will let you know when we are heading out."

Tommy was already in his basketball sneakers and draining three pointers with the other boys.

I sought out Coach Sampras.

"Hey Coach, how are you tonight?"

"Ready to practice! OO-RAH!"

Got to love military veterans.

"Perfect. Would you please lead the team in warm ups and our first few drills? I need to talk to Clay."

"You got it, Coach."

I could feel my stomach getting tight as I thought about what was to come. About how I have no training. How inadequate I felt for this task. How I could screw this up. But also, that I must do my best to help this child.

As the team began to practice I began to call a number of players over one at a time so that it was not obvious I was singling Clay out.

"Dean!"

"Yes, Coach?"

"Walk with me."

"Okay, Coach."

"Great game last Saturday. That last shot you blocked was a key to our win. Tonight, I would like to see you focus on both the block but also the path in which you direct the ball, much like a goalie in hockey. Make the save and direct the puck to a teammate to clear it. Make sense?"

"Yes, Coach."

And then …

"Mickey T!"

"Yes, Coach."

"Walk with me."

"Yes, Coach."

"Tonight, during the scrimmage, I want you to play Tommy man to man. I want to see you push him hard under the boards on both ends. I want to see you fight him for every ball. And I want you to show off your 'rip it' skills. Can you do that for me?"

"I will do my best. Tommy is great under the boards."

"And so are you. Now let's see you both get even better."

"You got it, Coach."

And then …

"Clay!"

"Yes, Coach?"

"Walk with me."

"Okay Coach."

We walked a bit further than the others as I directed Clay to the teacher's dining room.

"Have a seat, Clay."

"Okay, Coach."

"Clay, I wanted to talk to you."

"Yeah, Coach."

"I understand you have been smoking a lot of weed and enticing other players to do so too."

"Coach?"

"Listen to me, Clay. You mean a lot to me and my family. As does your family."

"I know, Coach."

"Good. Because I am saying this because we love you. Using marijuana is a bad thing. The marijuana of today is not like it was years ago. It is far more dangerous and can do great harm. I don't want to see you harmed, Clay. And I don't want to see any of your teammates harmed either."

"Coach …"

I waited but Clay did not finish his thought.

"Clay, here is the deal, tonight after practice you tell your mother what is going on or I will."

"But Coach. I will stop. You, your family, and the team mean more to me than weed. I will stop right now. I promise."

"I hear you, Clay. And I hope that is true. But that is not enough. As I said, you tell your mom, or I will … tonight."

Clay and I went back and forth many more times with me doing my best to stress how much he means to us and how dangerous marijuana is to a young person. It wasn't easy and every chance I got I prayed, "Please God, help me to say the right thing. Help me to not make things worse." And most of all, "Please help Clay. Please keep him safe. Please give him the strength to stop using. Please give him strength to talk to his mom. And please give her strength."

"Coach, I will tell my mom after practice tonight. I promise. I will."

"And you will stop smoking and enticing others?"

"Yes, Coach. The people in my life mean far more to me than any drug."

"I am proud of you, Clay. Let me know how your conversation goes."

I wanted to ensure that the conversation both took place and that I was available afterwards just in case I could be helpful somehow.

"I will coach. I will."

Chapter 22

Going Long

"Team, they are going to press us as soon as they have the opportunity …"

We had a very good rivalry going with the other Gorham High School recreation basketball team. The kids on each team all knew each other very well. As did the coaches. And winning the head to head matchup meant a lot to many.

This was our first game against them since we beat them the previous season, after getting down by eight points early on only to find out the wrong ball was being used to start the game.

This was also our first game against them since Clay had opted to no longer play for me the season following the discussion we had had relative to his drug use.

Today would be the first time I saw Clay in another uniform.

Samuel Johnson once said, "Hell is paved with good intentions." Each day I wonder what I have contributed to this fiery pit.

"Tom, you messed up again. You hurt another child," I said to myself as I passed by many of the parents congregated in the hallway and began a slow walk to the visitor's bench.

I felt my gut hollowing and my hands shaking as I peered across the gym and saw Clay with his new team, shooting his patented deadly short jump shot.

I swallowed hard as I thought about how I could have handled the situation differently.

"Morning, Coach."

"Good morning, David. Are you ready to dominate in the paint?"

"You know it!"

"Now that is what I want to hear."

As David walked onto the court to warm up I could feel my entire body seizing with anxiety as a wave of cold washed over me and to my core I began to shake.

Needless to say, I was not in a great state of mind to coach this morning.

"Coach …"

"Hey, Pete. Ready for today?"

"Of course, but first, Dean needs to tell you something."

"What's going on, Dean?" I asked as I turned to my starting strong forward.

"Coach, me and Gary," Gary is Dean's friend on another team, "went to watch two of the Windham teams play earlier today. During warm ups we noticed that one of the teams was short players." Then with a deep breath, "so we played in the game for them."

"You did what?" I immediately thought. And then still internally processing, "You played for another team? You broke league rules and played for another team and thus jeopardized our entire season?"

"Dean, you and Gary know that is against the rules, right?"

I couldn't believe what I was hearing. And here we were just a couple of minutes away from the tipoff of our game.

"Dean, go warm up."

"Yes, Coach."

"Tom, I couldn't believe it either. And I wanted you to know … and for Dean to tell you."

"Thanks, Pete." And then after thinking more, "I am not sure what the league will do. If we will need to forfeit all of our wins, if they will penalize us games, if they will suspend us. I am not sure. After the game I will inform the league director of what had happened. But for now, I am going to bench Dean. Perhaps me doing so (with him being one of our best players) will be punishment enough."

"Makes sense, Tom. I am sorry."

I was already not in great spirits and now this. But as they say on Broadway … "the show must go on."

"Bring it in!"

"Here is the starting lineup: Tommy at the 1, Mark at the 2, Bobby at the 3, Sully at the 4, and David at the 5."

Dean would typically be at the 4 (strong forward) and I would have Bobby coming off the bench. But not today.

"Team, they are going to press as soon as they have the opportunity to do so in order to try to bury us quick."

And then after pausing to look each of our starters in the eyes, "So here is what we are going to do…

We are going to set up the four, but Tommy, I want you and that cannon of an arm of yours passing the ball in. Bobby, when Tommy smacks the ball and yells 'BREAK!' I want you to set a screen for Sully. Sully, I want you to run through the screen and go long. Tommy, fake the inbound pass to the right side to David and then launch a Brady-esque bomb over the defense. Sully, all you will need to do is catch the ball and then hit the layup. Let's make them rue the day they pressed us. Understood?"

"Yes, Coach!"

"Great ... Tommy ..."

"Gorham on 3, one, two, three ...", Tommy screamed over the sound of the crowd.

"GORHAM!!!!"

After the starters ran onto the court, I pulled Dean aside.

"Dean," I could feel my body shaking even more, "I am sitting you today. I don't know what the league will say about what transpired this morning so for the good of the team ... I am sitting you."

"Okay, Coach," came the dejected response.

The other Gorham team won the tipoff and, with its talented point guard driving hard to the hoop, scored the first two points of the game.

"PRESS! PRESS!! PRESS!!!"

Fred, the head coach of the other team, immediately called the press but Tommy was ready.

"SET UP! FOUR!" He called out to set the play.

The ref tried to give Tommy the ball, but Tommy was savvy enough to realize once he took it the five second clock would begin ticking. So, with our team not quite in position to run the play I just drew up, Tommy let the ball fall from the ref's hands onto the court.

"That's it, Tommy!" I thought watching his gamesmanship.

And then, once our team was in position, Tommy accepted the ball from the ref and scanned the defense … as did I.

I noticed they had a full court press in place with no safety help. "Yes!" And I could see Tommy saw it too.

Tommy then smacked the ball and yelled, "BREAK!"

Bobby leaned into his man and then, using his forearm for leverage, ran away from him and into perfect position to set the screen for Sully.

Sully seeing this first faked away from Bobby to get his man off balance, and then cut back toward the screen.

When he did, he ran his defender straight into Bobby's pick, and with no switch and no safety help, Sully turned on the jets and went long.

Out of the corner of my eye I could see Fred yelling for someone to get back on defense as Tommy faked to his right and then reset and without moving his feet launched a bomb toward Sully who was now passing the half court line.

Tommy did not throw a high rising mortar mind you, but rather (as we say here in Maine) a frozen rope just over the defense and smack dab into Sully's hands as he reached the top of the key on the other end of the floor.

Sully, who is quite the athlete himself, caught the ball in stride and then with two dribbles laid the ball perfectly off of the backboard and into the basket for two points.

"Tied game," I heard Pete yell as I turned back toward Tommy and mouthed to him, "Perfect."

The other Gorham team never tried to press us again this day. Not with Tommy-Gun ready to go over the top with his cannon-like arm.

And yet ...

Without me placing Dean in the lineup, I unintentionally positioned our team to lose. Dean was a huge asset to our team, and even though the rest of the boys played with heart and fire … and did all they could to win … we didn't. We lost by eight to a better coached team.

"Great effort, Team. You gave it your all and I am very proud of you. You all showed heart and perseverance." And then after a pause as I glanced over and saw Clay heading into the stands to see his mother I continued, "I have much work to do to better position you all for the next game … beginning at our next practice … which is Tuesday night at 7:00pm at the Narragansett School. Any questions?"

"No Coach."

"Okay. Tommy …"

"Gorham on 3, …."

Then after calling Dean over to me I let him know, "I will speak to the league director and we will get this straightened out. I think having you sit today bodes well for us. And us losing today may as well." Which sounded awkward to say. "Do you understand why I sat you?"

"Yes, Coach."

Truth be told I am not sure that he did. And also, truth be told, I again am not sure that I did the right thing. As is said, "Hell is paved by good intentions."

After speaking with Dean and then Coach Sampras I packed up my bag and turned to find my family.

The stands were still emptying so it was not easy to find Doc, Sammy or Haylee immediately. But I did see Clay and his mom … and I knew I needed to go talk to them both.

"Tom!"

"There you are, Doc. I didn't see you or the girls."

"Why didn't you play, Dean? You guys would have won."

"A long story. I will tell you later. Right now, I want to talk to Clay and his mom."

"Hi Sandy."

"Hi Tom. Tough game, huh?"

"It sure was." And then turning to Clay, "Hey Clay. Good game."

"Thanks, Coach."

"You doing okay, son?"

"I am, Coach. I really am."

"I care about you. Our whole family cares about you."

"I know, Coach. I know."

"He is doing very well. Thank you, guys so very much."

"We love Clay," Doc replied to Sandy. And then to Clay, "You know we truly do, Clay. We truly do. And we miss you."

"I know you do."

As with all of the boys I have coached, I care deeply about Clay and think about him often. Coaching 'the Big Kid' has become more than a father trying to help his son, a son who had faced and overcome much adversity. It has become a life changing endeavor for me. A blessing in so many ways … and a curse.

As a coach, you are blessed with the opportunity to help change lives. To help a child grow on and off the court.

As a coach, you are also cursed with opportunities to do great harm. To make the wrong decision and harm the well-being of a child because you made a mistake.

Each day I wonder, which child did I help, and whom have I hurt.

"Hell is truly paved with good intentions."

Chapter 23

Retirement

Coaching young men's basketball ended for me after the 2014 season. The team (led by 'The Big Kid') had a tremendous year on the court with a last second loss in the semifinal game preventing us from competing for the championship.

Walking off the court that day I knew I was done with coaching (at least for the time being). Tommy was graduating, as was the core of our team. I was physically exhausted after having commuted to and from Boston from Maine for 2.5 years (rushing back to attend practices and games) and mentally exhausted after having faced my own limitations in an effort to lead and support young men for so long.

Over the next year or so I was asked by the head of the league to coach again and offered a coaching position with another school system (this time coaching young women) but in each instance I knew that the time was not right for me to pick up my whistle once more. My time was done.

Sometime later, many of the feelings I experienced while walking away from coaching arose as I stepped on the court to play basketball with my son Tommy, his friends (two of my former players), my former assistant coach, and another neighborhood young man.

For a good number of years this core group has been playing pickup basketball on Sunday mornings. The games are typically competitive. And when I was still coaching this was an opportunity to review game plans, technique, strategies, and more … and once I stopped coaching to simply play, get some exercise, have fun, and be together.

As time has passed, I have realized more and more that as I have aged my ability to keep up, to compete, and to walk away at the end of our two to four hours of playing still healthy has eroded.

And as of this particular day, I have decided to retire from also playing the game that I love.

Now admittedly, this isn't the first time I felt like this. In fact, two years prior, I wrote a poem titled "Passing the Rock" which expressed this same feeling.

Feed the rock … to the spot

Pass the torch … leave the court

Take a pause … to no applause

Retire the number … to the slumber

But this day was different. This day I experienced the worst of myself and I never want to experience it again.

The first game began inauspiciously enough. We had a three on three going and Kyle, the young man who I had not coached prior but who has played with us on Sundays a couple of times in the past, was driving toward the basket.

Seeing this I came off of my man, slid over to defend the penetration, and with my right hand attempted to poke the ball away from him.

But unfortunately for me, the ball ended up bouncing off of Kyle's thigh and right back into my right index finger with a pop and a crack.

(Yes, immediately I had a sense it was broken as the knuckle disappeared and the pain shot all the way into my wrist.)

And yet, this is street ball, I am from Brockton, and I was not about to tell anyone nor stop playing.

Or as Doc says, "You are being stupid again."

"Okay, Tom." This was my self-talk. "Knowing you cannot shoot with your left (never could) just use three fingers on your right hand to shoot and adjust your shot accordingly. The finger is broke, you popped it back into place, it is no longer dislocated … it will just be pain. Don't let your team down."

And of course, "It is what it is. Just play the game with your son et al and enjoy."

And that is what I did for the rest of the first game and into the second. I wasn't scoring much as Tommy, Phil, Justin and Kyle began to heat up and Pete owned the boards, but the game and a half were close.

At least until …

The boys Pete and I coached since they were about 9 years old are now 19 and 20. They are big, fast, agile, and strong (in addition to being very good basketball players).

The next week I would be 50. I am no longer fast and agile. And as for big … well let's not go there.

About midway through the second game, Tommy (who this time was on the other team) drove the lane much like Kyle did earlier. And much like earlier, I tried to slide over to cover the drive and ideally make a stop. But I was too slow and rather than getting in front of Tommy and in good defensive position, seeing that I was going to be late and would only cause a collision and a foul, I tried to back off.

Tommy was driving to the hole with abandon. He was driving with a purpose. And by the look in his eye he knew no one could stop him.

Unfortunately for me, I was slow, late and in his way. And as I turned away from Tommy we collided and immediately I felt my pelvis dislocate and my back seize up.

I was hurt. Not 'broken finger' hurt. I was really hurt. And I was ticked off. (Not something that I am proud of.)

I was ticked off at being old. I was ticked off at being slow. I was ticked off that I was in the way. I was ticked off I was a retread on the court. I was ticked off that I am no longer a good basketball player. And I was ticked off because I was really hurt.

Was it Tommy's fault? Absolutely not. He was playing basketball the way you should. With passion and confidence.

Did I tell anyone I was hurt? Absolutely not. I was too mad. And besides, what is telling anyone going to do?

So, what did I do?

Tommy scored on that play and it was now my team's ball. I knew I had no lateral movement, but I also knew I had a ton of adrenaline masking much of the pain I would feel later so …

On the inbounds play, and with the ball in my hands, I knew I could go straight, and with Tommy playing off of me (probably because he recognized my shot was even worse than usual) I thought I could get a couple of steps on him.

I also thought (and this I am also not proud of), "I will show you kid. You think you can drive on me. My turn!"

Yes, it was now my turn to drive with abandon to the basket thinking no one can stop me.

Boy was I wrong.

As I took my first two steps off the dribble, I saw Tommy stepping up to cover me. And with no lateral movement or speed to side step or spin away from Tommy, and with my adrenaline firing, I figured I would drop my shoulder, initiate contact, put up a shot, and if luck would have it net two points for our team.

But luck was not on my side. Rather, all I did was drop my shoulder, make contact, and watch my son, the boy (who is now 19 and bigger and stronger than me), fall backwards as I bounced to the side and lost the ball out of bounds.

I watched the boy, who has become a man, hit the hard court … and all I could think was "what have I done?"

Tommy got up immediately (thank the good Lord) and was fine.

I was not.

Right then I knew … it was over for me. Yes, I retired from coaching a couple of years ago. And right now, I was retiring from playing as well.

I am no longer good enough and this time I almost hurt my son.

"I am so sorry, Tommy."

Now, of course, you don't leave a series of games whether you have a broken finger or worse (we tend to say 'rub some dirt on it'). No. You play to the end. Yes. I was retiring, but I am not quitting. At least not until we are all done playing this day.

By game four or five I was essentially useless on the court but did have a good pass or two each game to maintain an ounce of pride here and there, but it was actually another collision that proved to be a benefit.

I believe it was a rebound both Tommy and I were going for when Tommy bowled me over like I was a child.

"Yes! Providence! Penance!" I thought as I rolled along the baseline. "That was payback for what I did earlier," I continued while recognizing that in reality it wasn't, and I have much to do to make up for almost hurting my son.

"Are you okay, Dad?"

"I'm good. Our ball," was what I responded.

Looking back now what I should have said was, "No, Tommy. I am not. I almost hurt you and I am sorry. Your father is greatly flawed. Always has been and always will be. I love you. The court is now yours."

So yes … my coaching days are over.

And now my playing days as well.

Will this retirement be a "Favre-ian" retirement …

… or like many a boxer …

… I cannot honestly say.

All I know is at this time I am retired from playing basketball.

This day I passed the rock for the last time … to a group of amazing, talented, and caring young men led by the Big Kid.

Today I extinguish one fire as a new and brighter flame burns on.

Chapter 24

The Love of Coaching

There were great learnings over the many years I coached young men's basketball.

Yes, hopefully by the young men I was blessed to lead, and yet even more so by me.

I came into coaching as perhaps many a father does … by simply wanting to support my son, the Big Kid.

And the journey was one of great mountains climbed and many valleys crossed.

There was blood, there was most assuredly sweat, and there were many a tear. And yet today I look back at amazing young men finding their path and I am ever so proud of each.

If you think coaching is just about X's and O's, you are either not fully engaged as a coach, or simply never had the opportunity to open your heart to the fullest.

Coaching allows you to impact a life in some of the most powerful and profound ways.

- A young man dealing with body image issues.

- A young man struggling as his parents' divorce.

- A young man rejected by the many teams he approached.

- A young man neglected by his parents.

- A young man experimenting with drugs.

- Young men trying to prove themselves in a society that provides mixed messages as to what a young man should be.

- A young man bullied by adults (other coaches, teachers, neighbors).

- A young man learning about death and dying as his mother fights heroically her battle with cancer before succumbing to the disease.

- Young men wanting to feel wanted, wanting to find their place, their community, their home.

The X's and O's were the easy part.

Leading, mentoring, parenting, coaching these young men through these challenges when at times they love you and other times they hate you ... all the while you are loving them ... now that is the Heart of Coaching.

Trying to live a life where you own your own frailty, your own mistakes, and each day, each game, still striving, still leading even when on occasion the face in the mirror wants to do something (anything) else because of the pain you yourself feel … now that is the Soul of Coaching.

- New substitution patterns to better position the team to win.

- Implementing new plays taking advantage of your team's strengths.

- Creating a new style defense to leverage what your players do best.

- Modifying and then running skill development drills to ensure both learning and fun.

- Simplifying and then implementing new offensive plays based on the best of the best in college and pro ball to keep the kids interested.

- Teaching, supporting, cheering, coaching.

Again … the easy part.

Comforting two young men as their father passes away suddenly … now that is the Engagement of Coaching.

And each day realizing you are on an island … simply a parent trying to help … making many mistakes … learning and growing … and hopefully serving and helping others … that is the Love of Coaching.

When I decided to step away from Coaching I knew that one day I would come back to basketball … in one form or another.

And no, not as a player.

And recently I did.

Not as a Coach this time. But rather as a team sponsor.

Yes, the sponsor of the Gorham High School Rec Basketball team … DHLG.

And to do so, I knew I needed to find a new Coach. A special Coach. A Coach who may be young and yet has the heart, mind, soul, and love of the game but even more so the love for helping others … and has done so all his life.

The first place I looked was to my son Tommy, The Lion. And yet, he was away at school and coaching these young men requires time.

Then I knew exactly who my team needed.

We needed another young man with …

- a track record of helping, supporting, caring about others

- integrity and compassion

- knowledge of the game and even more so knowledge of people

- maturity, dedication, perseverance

- and a Heart of a Tiger

And that is who I recruited … and that is who our team got … our new Head Coach … Lance Starward.

Lance is all the above and more … and the young men of DHLG will learn, grow, be cared for and cared about, will learn the game of basketball, and will learn the game of life.

Thank you, Lance, for carrying forth as Coach of DHLG.

Each day you inspire.

Each day you teach.

Each day you care.

Each day you love.

Each day you make this world a better place.

Chapter 25

Courage

The journey was amazing because of great kids, great parents, a great program, family support and involvement ... and of course Peter Sampras my assistant coach throughout.

I think of this at this time as I reflect on a picture of Coach Sampras and me.

The picture itself I found to be quite profound as the word *"COURAGE"* is visible over our heads.

Because you see, so many of the young men we coached showed such great courage as they faced incredible challenges off the court that far outweighed any challenges they faced on the court.

I am so proud of each of the young men who came through our program, how each of them faced their own challenges, how they got up each and every time they were knocked down ...

… and how together we became a community.

God truly blessed us.

And I am most grateful to have been part of this team.

Acknowledgements

I love book acknowledgements. As I read them I make note of the vast numbers of people who contribute to a message creation. I also relish the gratitude and as we know gratitude heals in and of itself.

Thank you to my bride, Darlene aka Doc. Her power animal is the black bear and she embodies this power as she cares for me, our children, our critters, and all she loves. Without Doc's love, support, wisdom and guidance this work of heart would not exist.

To my son, Tommy aka The Big Kid. Without his courage, strength, vulnerability, resilience, passion and caring for his friends and family, I would not have learned and grown as a coach and as a person. I am most grateful.

To my daughter Samantha. Sammy was bullied as a child and more recently after she had won the title of Miss Maine USA. She too has shown courage, strength and resiliency as she has pursued her passions and continues to lead a life leading and in service to others.

To my daughter Haylee. Haylee was bullied during her high school years and she too has overcome. Her inner strength and spirit are inspiring and by her actions and love for others she supports and saves many.

My good friend Rachel Riverwood is my truth. When I write, and it is lousy, she tells me. And she does so with kindness and compassion. She is a true friend who I respect and adore.

Kristin Walker defines the term genuine. Kristin, through her Mental Health News Radio Network and through her friendship, has inspired many a deep discussion relative to bullying, narcissism, abuse and resiliency and has also taught me much.

The director of the Gorham Recreation Basketball program is a special young man by the name of Alan Grady. He provided me with the opportunity to become a head coach within this program which changed my life. Alan also ran a program with integrity and truly cared about the children. Yes, a special young man.

I am also so grateful for the other coaches throughout the league. Each coach investing time and energy and doing their best to help young men.
And each game I learned greatly from them.

Alan Bell is a Gorham coach who essentially became my mentor. He knows the game. But more importantly he cares about and invests in children.

Huge thank you to my number one assistant coach, Boris Becker. Through thick and thin, when I traveled, each and every practice, each and every game, and even Sunday pickup games … Boris was there. A rock. A sounding board. A calming presence. A special person who made each of us better.

And to my second assistant coach, Chris Erickson. A terrific father, coach and friend. Always with a kind word and key insight to better our team.

We would not have created the community that we did, that others gravitated to, without the parents of our players. I learned so much from so many.

To Faith. My bride's best friend who supported Doc and was always there for her and for our family. Faith is one of those Angel's on earth … and her name is so very fitting.

To my Dad, for loving me and never allowing me to take the easy way. For naming me Tommy Heinsohn. For teaching me the game of basketball. For showing me the love of the game. For playing basketball with me in our front yard and not taking it easy on me. For teaching me how to be a father.

To my Mom, for loving me unconditionally.

My brother Jon and sister Darlene were always better athletes and by watching them I also learned so much and am better for it.

To the referees who volunteered their time to ensure games were fair and children were safe. For becoming friends and for also teaching me the game.

To a special sponsor, John Toothaker, God rest his soul. Not only did John support our team financially, not only did he secure us gym time when needed, not only did he care deeply about his sons and his wife, he showed us all how to be love in action for others.

Tommy Heinsohn, Dave Cowens and Charles Barkley became role models for me and for the Big Kid and continue to impact us to this day. And an extra thank you to Dave Cowens and his wife who also took the time to come to one of our games.

Mike the custodian who joined our community and ensured our team always had a clean and safe place to practice. Who provided me with much needed coffee and became a true friend to me and the team.

Kay Kendall has been a key supporter of all my writing. She has edited one of my books and continues to help me become a better writer.

Mark Ridgeway is a coach's dream. He is the Tedy Bruschi of each and every one of his teams, leading, doing more than asked, teaching. Always positive and incredibly talented. He is also a tremendous coach and great friend to our family.

To my beloved pup, Gabriel. Always there by my side as I write. And always there each evening when I arrived home after a tough practice or game. Not judging. Just loving.

And to all the players who allowed me to coach them over the years. You each have a special place in my heart. You too have taught me, and I am truly a better coach and a better person because of each of you.

BONUS MATERIAL

10 Steps for Benching Bullying by Coaches

Noted in a Yale Rudd Center study, forty-two percent of children reported being bullied by physical education teachers and sports coaches. Another study found that 45 percent of children said, "their coaches called them names, insulted them or verbally abused them" and another study, this one from the United Kingdom, found that 25 percent of 6,000 young adults reported that they suffered emotional harm at the hands of their coaches.

Just think about that for a moment. Depending on the study, between 25 to 45 percent of our children who play sports are falling victim to a coach who is habitually cruel and abusing them. Up to almost half our children who play sports are being abused by coaches.

As Nancy Swigonski, MD, MPH, associate professor at Indiana University's School of Medicine, has noted in her piece in the journal *Pediatrics*, the damage these coaches are doing to our children is devastating and can be everlasting, "It can impair social and emotional development and cause substantial harm to mental health."

Clearly, there are many broader influences that affect children's health, and this certainly includes the bullying that happens on our ball fields that can lead to physical injury, social problems, emotional problems, mental health problems (e.g., depression, anxiety), and even death. Not to mention bullying can turn children off from physical activities and this can potentially lead to obesity.

So, what can parents do?

10 Steps to Bench Bullying by Coaches

1. Interview the coach and his/her staff. Ask about philosophy, priorities, playing time, values and how he/she measures the outcomes of each.

2. If your child is already on the team and you have concerns, ask your child about his/her experiences, the messages that are being sent, listen to understand and follow each path your child raises a concern about.

3. Inquire of other parents who currently or who previously had children on the team.

4. Look for red flags: According to Kody Moffatt, MD, a pediatrician in Omaha and executive committee member of the Council on Sports

Medicine and Fitness for the American Academy of Pediatrics, the number one red flag is a coach who wants "closed practices" where parents and other adults are barred from the practice. "That may be innocent, but as a pediatrician, a parent and a coach, I don't think any coach should tell an adolescent not to tell another adult something."

5. Be sure to attend (or perhaps rotate with other trusted adults) your child's practices.

6. If you notice bullying behavior, document it and include specifics.

7. Identify and map behaviors to team, school and/or league codes of conduct. Use this as a tool to share very specific examples of your concerns.

8. Address your concerns directly with the coach. Focus on the impact on the children and be specific.

9. If discussion with the coach is unsuccessful, reach out to the athletic director, school officials (if school-based program), and/or league officials, and share your findings.

NOTE: It is absolutely crucial to make note of how the coach is treating your child AND it is also critical to keep an eye out for how the other children are being treated as well. These are our communities and regardless of whom the child is, these behaviors are unacceptable, and it is incumbent upon us all to speak up for those who cannot do so for themselves and make a difference.

10. Ensure that you also focus on developing warm and trusting family relationships and positive home environments so that if your child is bullied the negative outcomes from the bullying will be minimized. According to the study "Families promote emotional and behavioural resilience to bullying: evidence of an environmental effort" published in the Journal of Child Psychology and Psychiatry, "Warm family relationships and positive home environments help to buffer children from the negative outcomes associated with bullying victimization."

Bullying by coaches is harmful and can lead to tragic ends. Together with these 10 steps we can identify it, stop it, mitigate its impacts, and help our children achieve their optimal health—physical, mental, emotional and spiritual.

PERSEVERE

Persevere
Never bend
Ignore the stare
Play till the end

No back down
Head held high
Support one another
Look 'em in the eye

Play with tenacity
Maturity and Grace
Play with integrity
No showboat ... no "in your face"

Great play from all
To dare, no shame
Go get that ball
Hit what you aim

The game is big
Life is bigger
Lead from the heart
Never surrender

BASKETBALL CATHARSIS

Heart driving
Courting life
Spotting treys
Facing strife

Minds melding
Hitting spots
Facing adversity
Drilling shots

Inspired pain
Stability shaken
Making move
Risk taken

Lion roars
Life begins
Inspiring son
Loss wins

Epilogue

Recently, Tommy and I were out on our deck and I assumed we were there for me to continue to actively listen and then prepare and provide sage words of wisdom.

Boy, was I wrong.

You see, Tommy has been on an incredible journey as of late. The Big Kid from The Big Kid and Basketball has tapped into his Heart … The Heart of the Lion … and has put into action his vision for a healthier self.

Physically he has surpassed many milestones … he has also done so mentally, emotionally, and spiritually.

His path has not been easy …

- He has lost old friends … and gained new ones,

- He has shunned God … and has also reconnected with the Almighty in an even more powerful way,

- But most of all … he has found his true authentic self.

So yes, we were on our deck and I was all ready to teach, to coach, to parent, to love … but it was not meant to be. For you see, this time, I was meant to once again learn, to be coached, to be loved. It was my turn to be humble, to admit frailty, to admit unknowing.

It was Tommy's time to lead, to serve, to love, and to teach his Dad.

And it was one of the most profound experiences of my life.

I learned much from my son and he provided me with a foundation in which I could carry forth and find my own path. And because of my son … I too am stronger physically, mentally, emotionally and spiritually.

Tommy – You are an inspiration to many, including your Dad (the old dog that learned a new trick).

Thank you for your courage.

Thank you for your heart.

Thank you for being vulnerable.

Thank you for being a leader.

Thank you for being love.

LOVE IS.

Author Bio

With well over thirty years of extensive leadership experience, Tom is a voice for relationship centered and compassionate loving care and servant leadership.

An author and advisor, he is also a nationally recognized speaker with an expertise in heart and mind communication, courageous vulnerability and bringing love into all we do.

Tom is a father, a husband and a coach. A coach to healthcare leaders. And a coach to young men.

He is also a poet. You can read his poetry on the WordPress site: The Uni-verse Within.

In his book *The Big Kid and Basketball* he shares stories of love, resiliency, parenting, coaching and family.

And be sure not to miss Tom's forthcoming novel, *From Heart to Head and Back Again … a journey through the healthcare system.* In this book you will see through his lenses as both a healthcare leader and as a patient who was told he would never work again and to get in line for a heart transplant. You will learn how together we can fan the flames of good in the system and how together we can also address its brokenness for the betterment of all.

"Abuse no one and no thing, for abuse turns the wise ones to fools and robs the spirit of its vision."

~ Chief Tecumseh

Made in the USA
Columbia, SC
30 August 2019